Pre-Algebra
Skill Building Workbook

with Explanations, Examples, Practice Problems and Answers

by
Stacy Otillio & Frank Otillio

ClayMaze.com

Copyright © 2023 - Stacy Otillio & Frank Otillio

All rights reserved.

TABLE OF CONTENTS

Section 1 - Negative Numbers
Addition, Subtraction, Multiplication and Division with Positive and Negative Numbers

1 - 8

Section 2 - Exponents
Positive Exponents, Negative Exponents, Roots

9 - 18

Section 3 - Factors, GCF & LCM
Divisibility Rules, Prime Factorization, GCF (Greatest Common Factor), LCM (Least Common Multiple)

19 - 30

Section 4 - Fractions
Equivalent Fractions, Simplifying Fractions, Mixed Numbers, Improper Fractions, Fraction Arithmetic

31 - 46

Section 5 - Decimals
Decimals and Place Value, Powers of 10, Converting Fractions and Decimals, Scientific Notation, Decimal Arithmetic, Percents

47 - 72

Section 6 - Expressions & Operations
Order of Operations (PEMDAS), Expressions and Variables, Combining Like Terms, Substitution, Laws of Exponents, Expanding and Factoring Expressions

73 - 106

Section 7 - Equations
One-Step Equations, Two-Step Equations, Combining Like Terms to Solve Equations

107 - 120

Section 8 - Points, Lines & the Coordinate Plane
The Coordinate Plane, Points, Lines, Distance Formula, Midpoint Formula, Slope, Intercepts, Linear Equations

121 - 154

Solutions
Answers to Problems - Sections 1-8

155 - 176

Negative Numbers

Addition, Subtraction, Multiplication & Division with Positive & Negative Numbers

Negative numbers are less than 0 and are written with a negative sign (-).

Positive numbers are greater than 0 and can be written with a positive sign (+) but are usually written with no sign.

Zero is neither positive nor negative.

On a number line, **negative numbers** appear to the **left** of **0** and **positive numbers** are to the **right** of **0**.

```
←——+——+——+——+——+——+——+——+——+——+——→
  -5  -4  -3  -2  -1   0   1   2   3   4   5
```

Below is another example of a number line, counting by 100's. The same idea applies:

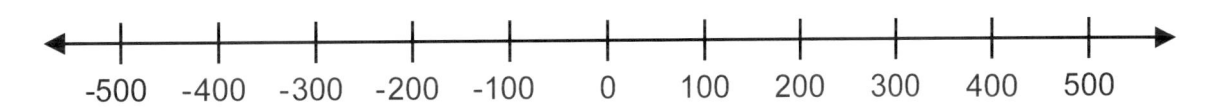

```
←——+——+——+——+——+——+——+——+——+——+——→
 -500 -400 -300 -200 -100  0  100 200 300 400 500
```

Unlike positive numbers, negative numbers with higher magnitudes are less than those with lower magnitudes. For example, 5 > 2, but -5 < -2.

Example: Compare the numbers.

-8 < 1   -8 is less than 1
0 > -6   0 is greater than -6
-2 < -1   -2 is less than -1

Example: Write the set of numbers in order from least to greatest: {3, -7, 0, 1, -4, -1}

-7 is the smallest (since it is negative and has the highest magnitude of the negative numbers in the group), followed by -4, and then -1. 0 is next, followed by 1 and then 3.

-7 < -4 < -1 < 0 < 1 < 3   Ordered Set: {-7, -4, 0, 1, 3}

ClayMaze.com

Name _____ Date _____

Negative Numbers

Fill in the blanks on the number lines with the missing numbers.

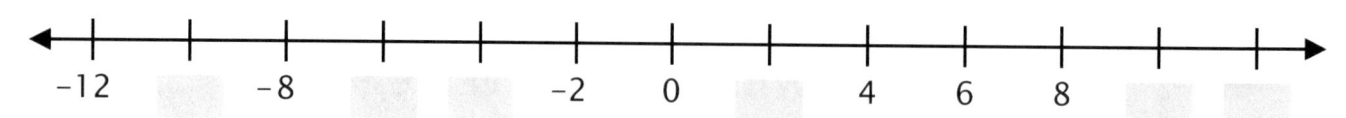

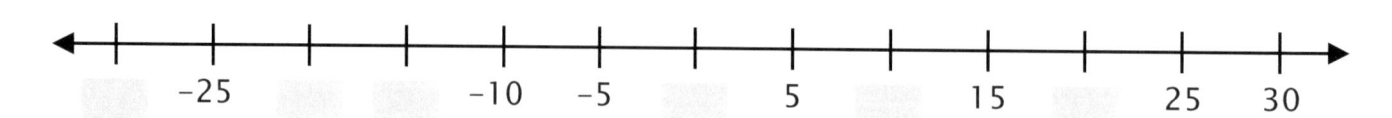

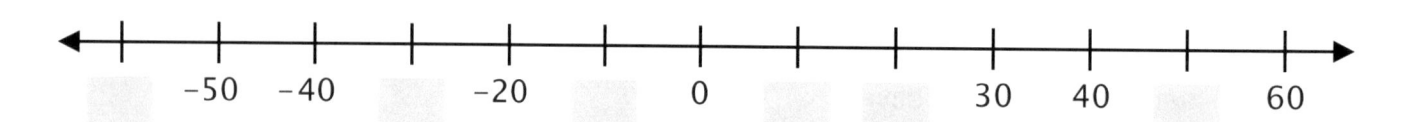

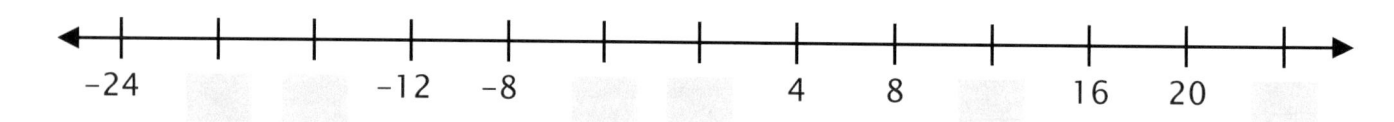

-12 ___ -8 ___ ___ -2 0 ___ 4 6 8 ___ ___

___ -25 ___ ___ -10 -5 ___ 5 ___ 15 ___ 25 30

___ -50 -40 ___ -20 0 ___ 30 40 ___ 60

-24 ___ ___ -12 -8 ___ ___ 4 8 ___ 16 20 ___

Compare the numbers in each pair and fill in the blanks with < or >.

1.   -2 ___ 0   2.   -12 ___ 11   3.   200 ___ -400

4.   50 ___ -52   5.   -14 ___ -13   6.   29 ___ -35

7.   -85 ___ -96   8.   27 ___ -84   9.   -112 ___ -55

10.   4 ___ -7   11.   0 ___ -1   12.   -34 ___ -35

Order the numbers in the sets from least to greatest.

1. {5, 6, -7, -3, 10, -12, 0} _____

2. {12, -19, 13, -12, 15, 3, -7} _____

3. {300, 0, -200, -500, 400, 800, 700} _____

4. {-44, 40, -65, -21, 80, -40, -62} _____

ClayMaze.com

Addition & Subtraction with Positive and Negative Numbers

Adding Numbers with Like Signs

When **adding only positive numbers**, the numbers are added together and the sum is **positive**.

When **adding only negative numbers**, the magnitudes of the numbers are added together and the sum is **negative**.

Example:

a. 5 + 7 = 12

b. −5 + −7 = −12

Adding Two Numbers with Different Signs

When adding two numbers with different signs, the smaller magnitude is subtracted from the larger magnitude and the result has the sign of the number with the larger magnitude.

Example: −7 + 5

Step 1: Subtract the smaller magnitude from the larger one: 7 - 5 = 2

Step 2: Determine the sign: -7 has the larger magnitude and it is **negative**, so the result is **negative**. -7 + 5 = -2

Subtraction

When subtracting a number from another number, we can rewrite the subtraction problem as an addition problem. Subtracting a positive number is the same as adding the negative of that number.

For example, -3 - 4 can be rewritten as -3 + -4.
Then the negative numbers are added: -3 + -4 = -7

Positive and Negative Signs next to Plus and Minus Signs

When there is a plus or minus sign next to the positive or negative sign of a number, the signs can be consolidated before calculating the answer.

Same signs (+ + or − −) ➡ plus (+)   Different signs (+ − or − +) ➡ minus (−)

Example: Add and Subtract.

Same signs:

a. 3 + +5 = 3 + 5 = 8

b. 3 − −5 = 3 + 5 = 8

Different signs:

c. 3 + −5 = 3 − 5 = −2

d. 3 − +5 = 3 − 5 = −2

Name _____   Date _____

Adding and Subtracting with Positive and Negative Numbers

Evaluate (Addition).

1. 3 + -57 _____
2. 53 + -2 _____
3. 1 + -99 _____
4. 13 + -2 _____
5. 14 + -2 _____
6. 98 + -6 _____
7. -2 + 8 _____
8. 5 + -45 _____
9. 1 + -39 _____
10. -2 + -8 _____
11. 10 + -1 _____
12. 8 + -28 _____
13. -17 + -6 _____
14. -93 + -1 _____
15. -19 + -6 _____
16. -6 + -98 _____
17. 17 + -6 _____
18. 5 + -75 _____
19. 18 + -6 _____
20. 6 + -89 _____
21. 9 + -29 _____

Evaluate (Subtraction).

1. -15 - 4 _____
2. 95 - -5 _____
3. 52 - -1 _____
4. -7 - 8 _____
5. -10 - 5 _____
6. 48 - 6 _____
7. 13 - -4 _____
8. 68 - -6 _____
9. 5 - -45 _____
10. 10 - 5 _____
11. 12 - 2 _____
12. 0 - -2 _____
13. -20 - -1 _____
14. 2 - 28 _____
15. 6 - 20 _____
16. 15 - -3 _____
17. -7 - 17 _____
18. -11 - 5 _____
19. 59 - -6 _____
20. 19 - -6 _____
21. -2 - -58 _____

Evaluate (Mixed).

1. 1 + -9 _____
2. 9 - -9 _____
3. 6 - -36 _____
4. -9 - 59 _____
5. -3 - 77 _____
6. -5 + 65 _____
7. 14 + -3 _____
8. 3 + -47 _____
9. 12 - -2 _____
10. -16 + 6 _____
11. -15 - 2 _____
12. 2 + -28 _____
13. 23 - 3 _____
14. 20 + 1 _____
15. 11 + -1 _____
16. -41 - -1 _____
17. 6 - -57 _____
18. 7 - -18 _____
19. 45 + 4 _____
20. -12 + 0 _____
21. 4 - -66 _____

ClayMaze.com

Name _____ Date _____

Adding and Subtracting with Positive and Negative Numbers

Evaluate (Addition).

1. 10 + -2 _____
2. 3 + -27 _____
3. 6 + -8 _____
4. 16 + -6 _____
5. -25 + -2 _____
6. -6 + -39 _____
7. -7 + 77 _____
8. -13 + -2 _____
9. -10 + -1 _____
10. -3 + 7 _____
11. 20 + -5 _____
12. 17 + -7 _____
13. -15 + 0 _____
14. -3 + 57 _____
15. 58 + -6 _____
16. 87 + -6 _____
17. -26 + 5 _____
18. 0 + -4 _____
19. -64 + 0 _____
20. 9 + -69 _____
21. 19 + -6 _____

Evaluate (Subtraction).

1. 12 - 15 _____
2. 8 - 28 _____
3. -3 - 17 _____
4. 0 - 4 _____
5. 11 - 0 _____
6. -58 - -6 _____
7. -12 - 1 _____
8. 58 - -4 _____
9. 1 - 59 _____
10. 14 - -5 _____
11. -11 - -1 _____
12. 13 - 3 _____
13. 3 - -47 _____
14. 10 - -4 _____
15. 7 - 98 _____
16. 15 - -2 _____
17. 7 - -9 _____
18. 11 - -1 _____
19. 16 - -6 _____
20. -3 - 67 _____
21. 29 - -5 _____

Evaluate (Mixed).

1. -6 + 8 _____
2. 13 - -2 _____
3. 4 - -96 _____
4. -23 + 2 _____
5. 28 - -1 _____
6. 82 - -7 _____
7. -44 + 0 _____
8. -3 + -7 _____
9. -5 - 55 _____
10. -83 - -3 _____
11. -18 + 6 _____
12. -1 - 29 _____
13. -13 + 1 _____
14. 6 + -49 _____
15. 2 + -64 _____
16. -1 + 79 _____
17. -8 - 19 _____
18. -15 - 4 _____
19. 19 - -6 _____
20. -10 + -4 _____
21. -3 + 27 _____

ClayMaze.com

Multiplication & Division with Positive and Negative Numbers

Multiplication

Same Signs
The product of two numbers with the same sign is **positive**.

Opposite Signs
The product of two numbers with opposite signs is **negative**.

Example: Multiply.

a. 7 x 2 = 14   positive x positive ⟶ positive

b. −3 x −4 = 12   negative x negative ⟶ positive

c. 5 x −7 = −35   positive x negative ⟶ negative

d. −4 x 2 x −3

    Multiply 2 numbers at a time. Let's start with the first two:

    (−4 x 2) x −3   −4 x 2 = −8, since the signs are opposite.

    −8 x −3 = 24   Both signs are the same, so the product is positive.

Division

Same Signs
The quotient of two numbers with the same sign is **positive**.

Opposite Signs
The quotient of two numbers with opposite signs is **negative**.

Example: Divide.

a. 40 ÷ 5 = 8   positive ÷ positive ⟶ positive

b. −21 ÷ −7 = 3   negative ÷ negative ⟶ positive

c. 12 ÷ −2 = −6   positive ÷ negative ⟶ negative

d. −32 ÷ 8 = −4   negative ÷ positive ⟶ negative

Name _____ Date _____

Multiplying and Dividing with Positive and Negative Numbers

Multiply.

1. -4 x -7 _____
2. -9 x -12 _____
3. 7 x 8 _____
4. -6 x -11 _____
5. 8 x 12 _____
6. 4 x 10 _____
7. -7 x -2 _____
8. -6 x -6 _____
9. -5 x -11 _____
10. -6 x 12 _____
11. 11 x -2 _____
12. 7 x -4 _____
13. -9 x 11 _____
14. 5 x -7 _____
15. -10 x -6 _____
16. 3 x -4 _____
17. -7 x 1 _____
18. -12 x 8 _____
19. -12 x -2 _____
20. -7 x -2 _____
21. -7 x -5 _____
22. -9 x -3 _____
23. 9 x -5 _____
24. 4 x -7 _____

25. -5 x -1 x -2 _____
26. -6 x -4 x -1 _____
27. 10 x -4 x -3 _____
28. -8 x -5 x -4 _____
29. -7 x 3 x -2 _____
30. -5 x -11 x -2 _____

Divide.

1. 8 ÷ 2 _____
2. 96 ÷ -8 _____
3. 48 ÷ -8 _____
4. -22 ÷ -2 _____
5. 5 ÷ -1 _____
6. -20 ÷ -4 _____
7. -15 ÷ -5 _____
8. -63 ÷ 9 _____
9. -54 ÷ -9 _____
10. 5 ÷ -5 _____
11. -88 ÷ 11 _____
12. 4 ÷ -2 _____
13. 16 : 2 _____
14. -18 ÷ -9 _____
15. 28 ÷ -7 _____
16. -45 ÷ -5 _____
17. 36 ÷ -12 _____
18. -48 ÷ -6 _____
19. -64 ÷ -8 _____
20. 2 ÷ -2 _____
21. 90 ÷ -9 _____
22. 110 ÷ -11 _____
23. -40 ÷ -5 _____
24. 132 ÷ -11 _____
25. 27 ÷ -3 _____
26. 24 ÷ -4 _____
27. -8 ÷ -4 _____
28. -33 ÷ -3 _____
29. 9 ÷ -3 _____
30. 108 ÷ -12 _____
31. 24 ÷ -3 _____
32. 70 ÷ -10 _____
33. -3 ÷ -1 _____

ClayMaze.com

Name _____ Date _____

Multiplying and Dividing with Positive and Negative Numbers

Multiply.

1. −2 x 5 _____
2. −10 x −8 _____
3. −3 x 11 _____
4. 12 x −10 _____
5. −4 x −5 _____
6. 2 x −6 _____
7. −2 x −11 _____
8. −5 x 6 _____
9. −12 x −12 _____
10. 2 x −8 _____
11. 12 x −2 _____
12. −5 x 12 _____
13. −8 x 7 _____
14. −8 x −2 _____
15. −2 x −2 _____
16. −10 x −9 _____
17. −10 x −10 _____
18. −7 x −7 _____
19. 3 x −10 _____
20. 5 x −11 _____
21. −3 x −12 _____
22. −5 x 5 _____
23. −7 x −3 _____
24. −2 x 4 _____

25. 6 x −7 x −1 _____
26. 10 x −9 x −1 _____
27. −2 x −5 x −3 _____
28. −3 x −4 x 2 _____
29. −7 x 5 x 2 _____
30. −11 x −2 x −4 _____

Divide.

1. −30 ÷ 6 _____
2. −50 ÷ 10 _____
3. 24 ÷ −6 _____
4. 72 ÷ −8 _____
5. −12 ÷ −2 _____
6. −12 ÷ −6 _____
7. −77 ÷ −7 _____
8. −84 ÷ −7 _____
9. −42 ÷ −7 _____
10. 120 ÷ −12 _____
11. −7 ÷ −1 _____
12. 50 ÷ −5 _____
13. −16 ÷ 2 _____
14. 10 ÷ −5 _____
15. 6 ÷ −2 _____
16. −22 ÷ −11 _____
17. −60 ÷ 12 _____
18. −48 ÷ −12 _____
19. −21 ÷ 3 _____
20. −27 ÷ 9 _____
21. 12 ÷ −3 _____
22. −4 ÷ 2 _____
23. −24 ÷ −12 _____
24. −14 ÷ 2 _____
25. −32 ÷ 4 _____
26. −44 ÷ 4 _____
27. −25 ÷ −5 _____
28. −15 ÷ −3 _____
29. 64 ÷ −8 _____
30. −20 ÷ −2 _____
31. −28 ÷ −7 _____
32. −12 ÷ −4 _____
33. 18 ÷ −9 _____

2 Exponents

Positive Exponents, Negative Exponents, Roots

An exponent indicates repeated multiplication of a number and is placed at the top right of the number. Below is an example of 4 raised to the power of 3 (or 4 to the third power). The number 3 is the exponent and the number 4 is called the **base**.

$$\text{base} \longrightarrow 4^3 \longleftarrow \text{exponent}$$

The 3 indicates that three 4's are multiplied together: $4^3 = 4 \times 4 \times 4$

Example: Evaluate.

a. 8^4

The base is 8 and the exponent is 4. The exponent indicates that **four** 8's need to be multiplied.

$$8^4 = \underbrace{8 \times 8}_{64} \times \underbrace{8 \times 8}_{64} = 64 \times 64 = 4{,}096$$

Note: Grouping the numbers two at a time can make the calculation easier.

b. −5 to the third power

When a number is raised to the third power it is said to be **cubed**. −5 to the third power (or −5 cubed) is written as $(-5)^3$. The base is −5 and the exponent is 3. The exponent indicates that **three** −5's need to be multiplied.

$$(-5)^3 = \underbrace{(-5) \times (-5)}_{25} \times (-5) = 25 \times (-5) = -125$$

Remember to pay attention to signs when evaluating exponents.
- If a negative number is raised to an even number, the result will be positive.
- If a negative number is raised to an odd number, the result will be negative.

ClayMaze.com

A number raised to the power of 1 is equal to the base number.
   For example, $4^1 = 4$

A number raised to the power of 0 is equal to 1.
   For example, $4^0 = 1$

Square: A number raised to the power of 2 is called the **square** of that number.

Cube: A number raised to the power of 3 is called the **cube** of that number.

Example: Evaluate.

a. 253^1

   If a number is raised to the power of 1, the result is the number.

   $253^1 = 253$

b. 29^0

   If a number is raised to the power of 0, the result is 1.

   $29^0 = 1$

c. Five squared

   Five squared is the same as 5 raised to the power of 2 and is written as 5^2. The base is 5 and the exponent is 2. The **2** indicates that **two** 5's need to be multiplied.

   $5^2 = 5 \times 5 = 25$

d. Two cubed

   Two cubed is the same as 2 raised to the power of 3 and is written as 2^3. The base is 2 and the exponent is 3. The **3** indicates that **three** 2's need to be multiplied.

   $2^3 = \underbrace{2 \times 2}_{4} \times 2 = 4 \times 2 = 8$

Name _____ Date _____

Exponents

Fill in the blanks using the appropriate form (word form, exponential form or expanded form):

	Word Form	Exponential Form	Expanded Form
1.	seven squared		7 x 7
2.		13^1	
3.	three to the fifth power		
4.			5 x 5 x 5 x 5 x 5 x 5 x 5
5.		11^5	
6.	eight to the eighth power		
7.			15 x 15 x 15
8.			4 x 4 x 4 x 4 x 4 x 4

Evaluate.

1. 3^2 = _____
2. 6^4 = _____
3. 2^0 = _____
4. 0^5 = _____
5. 12^3 = _____
6. 12^1 = _____
7. $(-3)^4$ = _____
8. 20^2 = _____
9. 1^5 = _____
10. $(-4)^5$ = _____
11. 9^2 = _____
12. $(-11)^3$ = _____
13. 0^3 = _____
14. 78^0 = _____
15. 16^1 = _____
16. 32^2 = _____
17. 200^2 = _____
18. 16^2 = _____

ClayMaze.com

Name _____   Date _____

Exponents

Fill in the blanks using the appropriate form (word form, exponential form or expanded form):

	Word Form	Exponential Form	Expanded Form
1.		3^7	3 x 3 x 3 x 3 x 3 x 3 x 3
2.	forty-four squared		
3.		5^5	
4.		100^4	
5.			14 x 14 x 14
6.	twelve to the fifth power		
7.	sixty-five to the fourth power		65 x 65 x 65 x 65
8.		24^2	

Evaluate.

1. 8^1 = _____
2. 17^2 = _____
3. 25^0 = _____
4. 13^2 = _____
5. $(-3)^5$ = _____
6. 9^4 = _____
7. 5^4 = _____
8. 50^2 = _____
9. 64^1 = _____
10. 3^0 = _____
11. 0^6 = _____
12. 2^6 = _____
13. $(-10)^4$ = _____
14. 300^2 = _____
15. 2^7 = _____
16. 8^3 = _____
17. 12^4 = _____
18. $(-40)^2$ = _____

ClayMaze.com

Negative Exponents

A positive exponent indicates repeated multiplication of the base number, but a **negative exponent** indicates **repeated multiplication of the reciprocal of the base.**

RECIPROCALS

The reciprocal is what you have when you "flip" a fraction by swapping the numerator and the denominator.

For example, the reciprocal of $\frac{2}{3}$ is $\frac{3}{2}$.

To write the reciprocal of an integer like 4, first change it to a fraction, then "flip" the numerator and the denominator.

4 is the same as $\frac{4}{1}$ and the reciprocal of $\frac{4}{1}$ is $\frac{1}{4}$.

So the reciprocal of 4 is $\frac{1}{4}$.

To change a number with a negative exponent to one with a positive exponent, change the base number to its reciprocal and then make the exponent positive.

For example, $4^{-3} = \left(\frac{1}{4}\right)^3$ This can also be written as: $4^{-3} = \frac{1}{4^3}$

This is because: $4^{-3} = \left(\frac{1}{4}\right)^3 = \frac{1}{4} \times \frac{1}{4} \times \frac{1}{4} = \frac{1 \times 1 \times 1}{4 \times 4 \times 4} = \frac{1}{4^3}$

When multiplying fractions, the numerators are multiplied together and the denominators are multiplied together.

In more general terms:

If n is a positive integer (1, 2, 3, 4, 5, ...) with $a \neq 0$ and $b \neq 0$:

$a^{-n} = \frac{1}{a^n}$ and $\left(\frac{a}{b}\right)^{-n} = \left(\frac{b}{a}\right)^n$

Example: Evaluate: 2^{-5}. *(First, change the expression into one with a positive exponent.)*

Using the rule from the previous page: $a^{-n} = \dfrac{1}{a^n}$

$$2^{-5} = \dfrac{1}{2^5} = \dfrac{1}{2 \times 2 \times 2 \times 2 \times 2} = \dfrac{1}{32}$$

Example: Evaluate: $(-8)^{-3}$

Using the rule from the previous page: $a^{-n} = \dfrac{1}{a^n}$

$$(-8)^{-3} = \dfrac{1}{(-8)^3} = \dfrac{1}{(-8) \times (-8) \times (-8)} = \dfrac{1}{-512} = -\dfrac{1}{512}$$

Example: Evaluate: $\left(\dfrac{1}{3}\right)^{-4}$

Change the base to its reciprocal to make the exponent positive: $\left(\dfrac{a}{b}\right)^{-n} = \left(\dfrac{b}{a}\right)^{n}$

$$\left(\dfrac{1}{3}\right)^{-4} = \left(\dfrac{3}{1}\right)^{4} = 3^4 = 81$$

Example: Evaluate: $\left(\dfrac{1}{5}\right)^{-3}$

Change the base to its reciprocal to make the exponent positive: $\left(\dfrac{a}{b}\right)^{-n} = \left(\dfrac{b}{a}\right)^{n}$

$$\left(\dfrac{1}{5}\right)^{-3} = \left(\dfrac{5}{1}\right)^{3} = 5^3 = 125$$

Name _____ Date _____

Negative Exponents

Evaluate.

1. 8^{-1}

2. 3^{-5}

3. $(-7)^{-2}$

4. 2^{-6}

5. $(-4)^{-3}$

6. 3^{-4}

7. 11^{-2}

8. $\left(\dfrac{1}{5}\right)^{-5}$

9. $\left(\dfrac{1}{2}\right)^{-4}$

10. $\left(\dfrac{1}{7}\right)^{-3}$

ClayMaze.com

Name _____ Date _____

Negative Exponents

Evaluate.

1. 10^{-3}

2. $(-8)^{-2}$

3. $(-2)^{-5}$

4. 3^{-1}

5. 7^{-4}

6. 16^{-2}

7. 5^{-4}

8. $(-1)^{-5}$

9. $\left(\dfrac{1}{10}\right)^{-4}$

10. $\left(\dfrac{1}{11}\right)^{-1}$

Roots

Square Roots

The square root of a number is the number which when squared equals the original number.

For example, the square root of 9 is 3, because $3^2 = 3 \times 3 = 9$.

The radical symbol $\sqrt{}$ is used to represent square roots.

  The square root of 9 is written as $\sqrt{9}$.

Note: There are actually two square roots: a positive number and the negative of that number. The positive square root of 9 is 3, but -3 is the other square root of 9 since $-3 \times -3 = 9$. However, for the purposes of this section, we will focus on the positive root, which is also known as the principal square root.

Cube Roots

The **cube root** of a number is the number which when cubed equals the original number.

The radical symbol with an index of 3: $\sqrt[3]{}$ is used to represent cube roots.

  For example, the cube root of 512 is written as $\sqrt[3]{512}$.

The cube root of a positive number is positive (the product of 3 positive numbers is positive) and the cube root of a negative number is negative (the product of 3 negative numbers is negative).

Example: Evaluate $\sqrt[3]{512}$ and $\sqrt[3]{-512}$

  To get the **cube root** of 512, we need to find a number which when **cubed** equals 512.

  $512 = 8 \times 8 \times 8$ or 8^3, so the cube root of 512 is 8: $\sqrt[3]{512} = 8$.

  To get the **cube root** of -512, we need to find a number which when **cubed** equals -512.

  $-512 = -8 \times -8 \times -8$ or $(-8)^3$, so the cube root of -512 is -8: $\sqrt[3]{-512} = -8$.

Name _____ Date _____

Roots

Evaluate.

1. $\sqrt{4}$

2. $\sqrt{64}$

3. $\sqrt{25}$

4. $\sqrt{16}$

5. $\sqrt{81}$

6. $\sqrt{121}$

7. $\sqrt{144}$

8. $\sqrt{1}$

9. $\sqrt{49}$

10. $\sqrt{100}$

11. $\sqrt{36}$

12. $\sqrt{0}$

13. $\sqrt{400}$

14. $\sqrt{900}$

15. $\sqrt[3]{8}$

16. $\sqrt[3]{-1}$

17. $\sqrt[3]{64}$

18. $\sqrt[3]{-125}$

19. $\sqrt[3]{-27}$

20. $\sqrt[3]{1,000}$

Factors, GCF & LCM

Divisibility Rules, Prime Factorization, GCF, LCM

Factors & Divisibility Rules

A **factor** is a number that divides evenly into another number <u>with no remainder</u>.

Integers greater than 1, whose **only** factors are itself and 1, are called **prime numbers**.

Example: What are the factors of 6? Is it a prime number?

6 is divisible by **1** and **6**, and also by **2** and **3**.
The factors of 6 are: 1, 2, 3 and 6. It is **not** a prime number.

Below are **divisibility rules** that can help with finding factors of numbers:

Divisible by: If:

2   the number is even (the last digit of the number ends in 0, 2, 4, 6 or 8)

3   the sum of the digits in the number is divisible by 3

4   the number formed by the last 2 digits is divisible by 4
   Note: 4 = 2x2, so if a number is not divisible by 2, then it is not divisible by 4.

5   the last digit of the number is either 0 or 5

6   the number is divisible by both 2 and 3

8   the number formed by the last 3 digits is divisible by 8
   Note: 8 = 4x2, so if a number is not divisible by 4, then it is not divisible by 8.

9   the sum of the digits in the number is divisible by 9
   Note: 9 = 3x3, so if a number is not divisible by 3, then it is not divisible by 9.

10   the last digit of the number is 0

There is a rule for 7, but due to its complexity, it's usually faster to just test by division.

Example: Test the divisibility rules (2 through 10) on the number 5,480.

- ✓ 2 – yes: 5,480 is an even number.
- 3 – no: 5+4+8+0 = 17, which is not divisible by 3.
- ✓ 4 – yes: The number formed by the last 2 digits is 80, which is divisible by 4.
- ✓ 5 – yes: The last digit of the number is 0.
- 6 – no: 5,480 is not divisible by 3, so it's not divisible by 6.
- 7 – no: 5,480 ÷ 7 = 782 with a remainder of 6. It does not divide evenly.
- ✓ 8 – yes: The number formed by the last 3 digits is 480, which is divisible by 8.
- 9 – no: 5+4+8+0 = 17, which is not divisible by 9. (Also, since it's not divisible by 3, it's not divisible by 9.)
- ✓ 10 – yes: The last digit of the number is 0.

Finding Factors of a Number

Find the first half of a number's factors by testing for divisibility up to the square root of that number. If the given number is not a perfect square (like: $2^2 = 4$, $3^2 = 9$, $4^2 = 16$, etc.), test up to the square root of the closest perfect square that occurs before the given number.

The rest of the factors are determined by dividing the given number by these factors.

Example: Find the factors of 75.

Step 1: Figure out how high to test for factors:

75 is not a perfect square, but the closest perfect square before 75 is 64 (or 8^2). So we only need to test up to 8.

Step 2: Use the divisibility rules to test through 8 (the number determined in Step 1).

We know 75 is divisible by 1, so that's a factor. ⟶ 1

75 is not even so it's **NOT divisible by 2, 4, 6 or 8**. Now let's test 3, 5 and 7:
7+5 = 12, which is divisible by 3, so 75 **is divisible by 3**. ⟶ 3
The last digit is 5, so 75 **is divisible by 5**. ⟶ 5
7 does not divide evenly into 75, so it's **not divisible by 7**

Step 3: Find the remaining factors. Testing through 8, we found that **1, 3 and 5** are factors. Dividing 75 by those numbers will give the rest of the factors:

1: 75÷1=75   Factors: 1, 75
3: 75÷3=25   Factors: 3, 25
9: 75÷5=15   Factors: 5, 15   **The factors of 75 are:** 1, 3, 5, 15, 25 and 75

Name _____   Date _____

Divisibility Rules & Factors

Circle the grey numbers that divide evenly into the given numbers in the left column.

1.	14	2	3	4	5	6	7	8	9	10
2.	135	2	3	4	5	6	7	8	9	10
3.	306	2	3	4	5	6	7	8	9	10
4.	1,620	2	3	4	5	6	7	8	9	10
5.	4,592	2	3	4	5	6	7	8	9	10
6.	25,238	2	3	4	5	6	7	8	9	10

List the factors of the numbers below. If a given number is prime, write prime.

7. 12

8. 64

9. 51

10. 65

11. 121

12. 70

13. 32

14. 47

Name _____   Date _____

Divisibility Rules & Factors

Circle the grey numbers that divide evenly into the given numbers in the left column.

1.	45	2	3	4	5	6	7	8	9	10
2.	175	2	3	4	5	6	7	8	9	10
3.	316	2	3	4	5	6	7	8	9	10
4.	1,744	2	3	4	5	6	7	8	9	10
5.	5,420	2	3	4	5	6	7	8	9	10
6.	45,950	2	3	4	5	6	7	8	9	10

List the factors of the numbers below. If a given number is prime, write prime.

7. 9

8. 54

9. 60

10. 36

11. 29

12. 15

13. 125

14. 100

22

ClayMaze.com

Prime Factorization

A **prime factor** is a factor that is a prime number.

Remember, prime numbers are whole numbers greater than 1 whose only factors are 1 and itself. Some examples of prime numbers are: 2, 3, 5, 7, 11, 13, 17, 19, ...

We can break numbers down into prime factors using repeated division by prime numbers until only a prime number remains.

Example: Write the prime factorization of 36.

Choose the smallest prime factor of the number and divide. Repeat this process on the quotients until the quotient is a prime number.

2 ⎵ 36	The smallest prime factor of 36 is 2, so divide by 2.	(36÷2=18)
2 ⎵ 18	The smallest prime factor of 18 is 2, so divide by 2.	(18÷2=9)
3 ⎵ 9	The smallest prime factor of 9 is 3, so divide by 3.	(9÷3=3)
3	3 is prime, so stop dividing here.	

The original number (36) is the product of the prime numbers that were extracted by the division and we can write:

$$36 = \underbrace{2 \times 2}_{2^2} \times \underbrace{3 \times 3}_{3^2} = 2^2 \times 3^2 \qquad \text{Prime factorization of 36: } \underline{2^2 \times 3^2}$$

Example: Write the prime factorization of 525.

Choose the smallest prime factor of the number and divide. Repeat this process on the quotients until the quotient is a prime number.

3 ⎵ 525	The smallest prime factor of 525 is 3, so divide by 3.	(525÷3=175)
5 ⎵ 175	The smallest prime factor of 175 is 5, so divide by 5.	(175÷5=35)
5 ⎵ 35	The smallest prime factor of 35 is 5, so divide by 5.	(35÷5=7)
7	7 is prime, so stop dividing here.	

The original number (525) is the product of the prime numbers that were extracted by the division and we can write:

$$525 = 3 \times \underbrace{5 \times 5}_{5^2} \times 7 = 3 \times 5^2 \times 7 \qquad \text{Prime factorization of 525: } \underline{3 \times 5^2 \times 7}$$

Name _____ Date _____

Prime Factorization

Write the prime factorization of the following numbers in the blanks below.

1. 12

2. 24

3. 25

_____ _____ _____

4. 75

5. 64

6. 21

_____ _____ _____

7. 51

8. 100

9. 57

_____ _____ _____

10. 120

11. 84

12. 125

_____ _____ _____

Greatest Common Factor (GCF)

The Greatest Common Factor (GCF) of two or more numbers is the largest factor shared by those numbers.

To find the GCF, first find the factors of each number, then select the largest factor that is shared by the given numbers.

Example: Find the GCF of 35 and 40.

First, find the factors of each number.

Factors of 35:   1   5   7   35

Factors of 40:   1   2   4   5   8   10   20   40

The largest factor shared by both 35 and 40 is 5, so **the GCF of 35 and 40 is 5.**

This same method can be applied to more than 2 numbers.

Example: Find the GCF of 12, 36 and 72.

First, find the factors of each number.

Factors of 12:   1   2   3   4   6   12

Factors of 36:   1   2   3   4   6   9   12   18   36

Factors of 72:   1   2   3   4   6   8   9   12   18   24   36   72

The largest factor shared by 12, 36 and 72 is 12, so **the GCF is 12.**

Sometimes it can be faster to first select the smallest number of the given numbers and see if that number divides evenly into the others. If so, it is the GCF.

In the example above, 12 is the smallest and it divides evenly into the other two: 36 and 72. If 12 had been tested first, we would have determined that it is the GCF, and the factoring steps could have been skipped.

Name _____   Date _____

Greatest Common Factor (GCF)

Find the GCF.

1. 16, 18

    GCF: _____

2. 35, 21

    GCF: _____

3. 24, 36

    GCF: _____

4. 54, 36

    GCF: _____

5. 10, 55

    GCF: _____

6. 21, 27

    GCF: _____

7. 54, 25

    GCF: _____

8. 56, 120

    GCF: _____

9. 70, 140

    GCF: _____

10. 42, 30

    GCF: _____

11. 24, 12, 45

    GCF: _____

12. 60, 24, 36

    GCF: _____

Name _____ Date _____

Greatest Common Factor (GCF)

Find the GCF.

1. 20, 24

   GCF: _____

2. 12, 8

   GCF: _____

3. 45, 30

   GCF: _____

4. 25, 75

   GCF: _____

5. 13, 26

   GCF: _____

6. 121, 77

   GCF: _____

7. 24, 90

   GCF: _____

8. 33, 15

   GCF: _____

9. 56, 49

   GCF: _____

10. 39, 24

    GCF: _____

11. 8, 48, 16

    GCF: _____

12. 60, 120, 85

    GCF: _____

Least Common Multiple (LCM)

The **Least Common Multiple (LCM)** of two or more numbers is the smallest number that is divisible by those numbers.

Finding the LCM of Two Numbers

One method of finding the LCM of two numbers is the following:

First, check if the smaller number divides evenly into the larger number (with no remainder). If so, that larger number is the LCM.

If the first step fails, start by multiplying the larger number by 2 and see if the smaller number also divides into that product. If not, test by multiplying by 3, then 4, then 5, etc. until a number is found that is divisible by both of the given numbers.

Example: Find the LCM of 5 and 25.

   First, see if the smaller number divides evenly into the larger number.

      The smaller number is 5, and it divides evenly into 25.

      Therefore, the **LCM of 5 and 25 is 25.**

Example: Find the LCM of 6 and 8.

   First, see if the smaller number divides evenly into the larger number.

      The smaller number is 6 and it does NOT divide evenly into 8, so 8 is not the LCM.

   Test multiples of the largest number (8). Start by multiplying by 2.

      8 x 2 = 16   16 is NOT divisible by 6, so test by multiplying by 3.

      8 x 3 = 24   24 IS divisible by 6. **The LCM of 6 and 8 is 24.**

This same method can also be used with 3 numbers.

Example: Find the LCM of 10, 4 and 8.

   First, see if both of the smaller numbers divide evenly into the largest number.

      The largest number is 10, which is not divisible by 4 or 8, so it's not the LCM.

   Test multiples of the largest number (10). Start by multiplying by 2.

      10 x 2 = 20   20 is divisible by 4 but not by 8, so test by multiplying by 3.

      10 x 3 = 30   30 is not divisible by 4 or 8, so test by multiplying by 4.

      10 x 4 = 40   40 IS divisible by 4, 8 and 10. **The LCM of 4, 8 and 10 is 40.**

Name _____   Date _____

Least Common Multiple (LCM)

Find the LCM.

1. 6, 12

   LCM: _____

2. 4, 6

   LCM: _____

3. 3, 7

   LCM: _____

4. 5, 20

   LCM: _____

5. 8, 10

   LCM: _____

6. 4, 50

   LCM: _____

7. 30, 9

   LCM: _____

8. 3, 4

   LCM: _____

9. 12, 5

   LCM: _____

10. 6, 15

    LCM: _____

11. 12, 4, 8

    LCM: _____

12. 5, 3, 6

    LCM: _____

Name _____   Date _____

Least Common Multiple (LCM)

Find the LCM.

1. 7, 2

    LCM: _____

2. 30, 12

    LCM: _____

3. 15, 45

    LCM: _____

4. 4, 10

    LCM: _____

5. 25, 3

    LCM: _____

6. 12, 18

    LCM: _____

7. 18, 36

    LCM: _____

8. 20, 6

    LCM: _____

9. 25, 4

    LCM: _____

10. 24, 36

    LCM: _____

11. 4, 5, 8

    LCM: _____

12. 6, 12, 20

    LCM: _____

Fractions

Equivalent Fractions, Simplifying Fractions, Mixed Numbers, Improper Fractions, Fraction Arithmetic

Equivalent Fractions

Equivalent fractions are fractions that have the same value with different numerators and denominators.

For example, $\dfrac{1}{2}$ is the same as $\dfrac{2}{4}$ and $\dfrac{3}{6}$.

To get an equivalent fraction, both the numerator and the denominator can be multiplied or divided by the same number.

Example: Find the missing values that make the fractions equivalent.

a. $\dfrac{4}{5} = \dfrac{?}{15}$

   The denominators are known in both fractions: 5 and 15

   Multiplying by 3 changes the denominator of 5 into 15, so the numerator must also be multiplied by 3 to get an equivalent fraction.

   $\dfrac{4\,(\times 3)}{5\,(\times 3)} = \dfrac{12}{15}$ The missing numerator is 12.

b. $\dfrac{7}{?} = \dfrac{35}{40}$

   The numerators are known in both fractions: 7 and 35

   Dividing by 5 changes the numerator of 35 into 7, so the denominator must also be divided by 5 to get an equivalent fraction.

   $\dfrac{7}{8} = \dfrac{35\,(\div 5)}{40\,(\div 5)}$ The missing denominator is 8.

Name _____   Date _____

Equivalent Fractions

Fill in each blank with the missing numerator or denominator to make the fractions equivalent.

1. $\dfrac{6}{} = \dfrac{12}{50}$ 2. $\dfrac{8}{10} = \dfrac{}{90}$ 3. $\dfrac{4}{} = \dfrac{20}{40}$

4. $\dfrac{4}{} = \dfrac{28}{77}$ 5. $\dfrac{8}{9} = \dfrac{}{18}$ 6. $\dfrac{}{25} = \dfrac{18}{50}$

7. $\dfrac{7}{8} = \dfrac{}{64}$ 8. $\dfrac{8}{} = \dfrac{56}{77}$ 9. $\dfrac{8}{} = \dfrac{64}{72}$

10. $\dfrac{6}{8} = \dfrac{30}{}$ 11. $\dfrac{}{8} = \dfrac{21}{24}$ 12. $\dfrac{6}{100} = \dfrac{18}{}$

13. $\dfrac{}{12} = \dfrac{27}{36}$ 14. $\dfrac{}{25} = \dfrac{15}{75}$ 15. $\dfrac{8}{25} = \dfrac{32}{}$

16. $\dfrac{6}{10} = \dfrac{}{40}$ 17. $\dfrac{5}{9} = \dfrac{25}{}$ 18. $\dfrac{}{12} = \dfrac{16}{48}$

19. $\dfrac{}{25} = \dfrac{28}{100}$ 20. $\dfrac{8}{22} = \dfrac{32}{}$ 21. $\dfrac{9}{25} = \dfrac{}{100}$

22. $\dfrac{4}{5} = \dfrac{12}{}$ 23. $\dfrac{}{10} = \dfrac{54}{60}$ 24. $\dfrac{8}{} = \dfrac{24}{60}$

25. $\dfrac{5}{} = \dfrac{15}{36}$ 26. $\dfrac{5}{6} = \dfrac{}{42}$ 27. $\dfrac{4}{12} = \dfrac{}{48}$

28. $\dfrac{}{10} = \dfrac{20}{50}$ 29. $\dfrac{4}{7} = \dfrac{20}{}$ 30. $\dfrac{5}{9} = \dfrac{25}{}$

ClayMaze.com

Simplifying Fractions

The numerator and denominator of a **simplified fraction** have no common factors other than 1.

To simplify a fraction, it's often fastest to find the GCF of the numerator and the denominator, and then divide them both by that number.

Alternatively, if you can't find the GCF quickly, the numerator and the denominator can be incrementally divided by common factors until there are none left.

Example: Simplify the fractions.

a. $\dfrac{12}{18}$ The GCF of 12 and 18 is 6.
To simplify, divide both the numerator and the denominator by the GCF (6):

$$\dfrac{12(\div 6)}{18(\div 6)} = \dfrac{2}{3}$$

b. $\dfrac{21}{35}$ The GCF of 21 and 35 is 7.
To simplify, divide both the numerator and the denominator by the GCF (7):

$$\dfrac{21(\div 7)}{35(\div 7)} = \dfrac{3}{5}$$

Example: Simplify $\dfrac{180}{255}$.

With this fraction, the GCF of the numerator and the denominator may not be immediately apparent, so we can find a smaller common factor to start with.

180 and 255 are divisible by 5, so 5 is a common factor that both can be divided by to reduce the fraction by a bit.

$$\dfrac{180(\div 5)}{255(\div 5)} = \dfrac{36}{51}$$

36 and 51 are divisible by 3, which is their GCF.

Divide both the numerator and the denominator by 3:

$$\dfrac{36(\div 3)}{51(\div 3)} = \dfrac{12}{17}$$

Name _____ Date _____

Simplifying Fractions

Simplify the fractions.

1. $\dfrac{2}{6} =$

2. $\dfrac{16}{20} =$

3. $\dfrac{18}{75} =$

4. $\dfrac{8}{100} =$

5. $\dfrac{6}{12} =$

6. $\dfrac{40}{55} =$

7. $\dfrac{36}{45} =$

8. $\dfrac{72}{80} =$

9. $\dfrac{24}{30} =$

10. $\dfrac{24}{28} =$

11. $\dfrac{18}{50} =$

12. $\dfrac{10}{25} =$

13. $\dfrac{140}{200} =$

14. $\dfrac{180}{360} =$

15. $\dfrac{256}{512} =$

ClayMaze.com

Improper Fractions & Mixed Numbers

An **improper fraction** is a fraction whose numerator is larger than its denominator.

A **mixed number** consists of a whole number and a proper fraction.

For example, $\frac{3}{2}$ is an improper fraction, and $1\frac{1}{2}$ is an equivalent mixed number.

Converting an Improper Fraction to a Mixed Number

Step 1: Divide the numerator by the denominator, noting the remainder and quotient.

Step 2: Form the mixed number using the results from Step 1.
   a. The whole number will be the quotient found in Step 1.
   b. The numerator of the fraction part will be the remainder found in Step 1.
   c. The denominator will stay the same.

Example: Convert $\frac{11}{5}$ to a mixed number.

Step 1:
Divide the numerator by the denominator.

$11 \div 5 = 2$ with remainder of 1.

$$\begin{array}{r} 2\ \text{R1} \\ 5\overline{)11} \\ \underline{10} \\ 1 \end{array}$$

Step 2:
A The whole number will be the quotient (2).

B The numerator of the fraction part will be the remainder (1).

C The denominator (5) will stay the same.

$$\frac{11}{5} = 2\frac{1}{5}$$

A → 2 (whole number)
B → 1 (numerator)
C → 5 (denominator)

Converting a Mixed Number to an Improper Fraction

Step 1: Find the **numerator of the improper fraction**: Multiply the denominator of the fraction by the whole number part and add that to the original numerator.

Step 2: The **denominator of the improper fraction** will be the same as the denominator of the fraction in the original mixed number.

Example: Convert the mixed numbers to improper fractions.

a. $2\frac{3}{8}$

   Step 1: Multiply the denominator by the whole number and add that to the numerator.

   denominator: 8   whole number: 2   numerator: 3

   denominator x whole number = 8 x 2 = 16

   16 + numerator = 16 + 3 = 19

   The new numerator will be 19.

   Step 2: The denominator is the same as the original denominator, which is 8.

   $2\frac{3}{8} = \frac{19}{8}$

b. $3\frac{1}{5}$

   Step 1: Multiply the denominator by the whole number and add that to the numerator.

   denominator: 5   whole number: 3   numerator: 1

   denominator x whole number = 5 x 3 = 15

   15 + numerator = 15 + 1 = 16

   The new numerator will be 16.

   Step 2: The denominator is the same as the original denominator, which is 5.

   $3\frac{1}{5} = \frac{16}{5}$

Name _____   Date _____

Improper Fractions & Mixed Numbers

Convert the improper fractions to mixed numbers.

1. $\dfrac{16}{7}$ 2. $\dfrac{37}{5}$ 3. $\dfrac{9}{2}$

   _____   _____   _____

4. $\dfrac{57}{23}$ 5. $\dfrac{45}{11}$ 6. $\dfrac{35}{6}$

   _____   _____   _____

7. $\dfrac{44}{5}$ 8. $\dfrac{7}{2}$ 9. $\dfrac{67}{8}$

   _____   _____   _____

10. $\dfrac{7}{5}$ 11. $\dfrac{71}{8}$ 12. $\dfrac{57}{41}$

    _____   _____   _____

13. $\dfrac{22}{3}$ 14. $\dfrac{26}{7}$ 15. $\dfrac{79}{15}$

    _____   _____   _____

ClayMaze.com

Name _____   Date _____

Improper Fractions & Mixed Numbers

Convert the mixed numbers to improper fractions.

1. $1\frac{4}{5}$

2. $5\frac{5}{9}$

3. $2\frac{3}{11}$

4. $2\frac{9}{25}$

5. $4\frac{4}{15}$

6. $6\frac{2}{3}$

7. $5\frac{7}{10}$

8. $3\frac{3}{25}$

9. $2\frac{3}{4}$

10. $4\frac{3}{20}$

11. $2\frac{5}{14}$

12. $3\frac{5}{8}$

13. $4\frac{5}{6}$

14. $8\frac{3}{7}$

15. $3\frac{7}{22}$

ClayMaze.com

Fraction Addition & Subtraction

When adding or subtracting fractions, the denominators should be the same.

To add (or subtract) fractions with the same denominators, the numerators are added (or subtracted) and the denominator stays the same.

Example: Add and subtract.

a. $\dfrac{1}{5} + \dfrac{3}{5} = \dfrac{1+3}{5} = \dfrac{4}{5}$

b. $\dfrac{5}{7} - \dfrac{2}{7} = \dfrac{5-2}{7} = \dfrac{3}{7}$

If the denominators are **different**, one or both of the fractions must be changed to an equivalent fraction so that both fractions have the same denominator. **The LCM of the denominators can be used as a good common denominator.**

Example: Evaluate.

a. $\dfrac{4}{5} + \dfrac{1}{10}$ Since these have two different denominators (5 and 10), their LCM should be found to use as a common denominator.

Step 1: Find a common denominator. The LCM of 5 and 10 is 10, so both fractions should have 10 as the denominator.

Step 2: Find equivalent fractions with common denominators. The only fraction that needs to change is $\dfrac{4}{5}$, since the second fraction's denominator is already 10.

So, we need to convert $\dfrac{4}{5}$ to an equivalent fraction with 10 as the denominator.

$\dfrac{4}{5} = \dfrac{?}{10}$ Multiply the numerator and the denominator by 2 to get a fraction with 10 as the denominator.

$\dfrac{4\,(\times 2)}{5\,(\times 2)} = \dfrac{8}{10}$

Step 3: Add the equivalent fractions with common denominators.

$\dfrac{4}{5} + \dfrac{1}{10} \longrightarrow \dfrac{8}{10} + \dfrac{1}{10} = \dfrac{8+1}{10} = \dfrac{9}{10}$

b. $\dfrac{5}{6} - \dfrac{1}{8}$ Since these have two different denominators (6 and 8), their LCM should be used as a common denominator.

Step 1: **Find a common denominator.** The LCM of 6 and 8 is 24, so both equivalent fractions should have 24 as the denominator.

Step 2: **Find equivalent fractions with common denominators.**

We need to figure out: $\dfrac{5}{6} = \dfrac{?}{24}$ and $\dfrac{1}{8} = \dfrac{?}{24}$

$\dfrac{5\,(\times 4)}{6\,(\times 4)} = \dfrac{20}{24}$ $\dfrac{1\,(\times 3)}{8\,(\times 3)} = \dfrac{3}{24}$

Step 3: **Subtract the equivalent fractions with common denominators.**

$\dfrac{5}{6} - \dfrac{1}{8} \longrightarrow \dfrac{20}{24} - \dfrac{3}{24} = \dfrac{20-3}{24} = \dfrac{17}{24}$

The same method can be used when adding more than two fractions. They all need to have the same denominator, which can be determined by finding the LCM of the original denominators.

Note: If you don't know the LCM, another common multiple can be used. However, using the LCM can save you more steps in simplifying, since you're dealing with smaller numbers.

Example: Find the sum: $\dfrac{1}{3} + \dfrac{1}{4} + \dfrac{1}{6}$

Step 1: **Find a common denominator.** The LCM of 3, 4 and 6 is 12, so the 3 equivalent fractions should have 12 as the denominator.

Step 2: **Find equivalent fractions with common denominators.**

We need to figure out: $\dfrac{1}{3} = \dfrac{?}{12}$ $\dfrac{1}{4} = \dfrac{?}{12}$ and $\dfrac{1}{6} = \dfrac{?}{12}$

$\dfrac{1\,(\times 4)}{3\,(\times 4)} = \dfrac{4}{12}$ $\dfrac{1\,(\times 3)}{4\,(\times 3)} = \dfrac{3}{12}$ $\dfrac{1\,(\times 2)}{6\,(\times 2)} = \dfrac{2}{12}$

Step 3: **Add the equivalent fractions with common denominators.**

$\dfrac{1}{3} + \dfrac{1}{4} + \dfrac{1}{6} \longrightarrow \dfrac{4}{12} + \dfrac{3}{12} + \dfrac{2}{12} = \dfrac{4+3+2}{12} = \dfrac{9}{12} = \dfrac{3}{4}$

Name _____   Date _____

Adding and Subtracting Fractions

Add the fractions and simplify.

1. $\dfrac{1}{2} + \dfrac{3}{8} =$ _____

2. $\dfrac{3}{7} + \dfrac{2}{3} =$ _____

3. $\dfrac{2}{5} + \dfrac{5}{6} =$ _____

4. $\dfrac{1}{2} + \dfrac{4}{5} =$ _____

5. $\dfrac{2}{3} + \dfrac{1}{5} + \dfrac{5}{6} =$ _____

Subtract the fractions and simplify.

6. $\dfrac{4}{5} - \dfrac{2}{3} =$ _____

7. $\dfrac{1}{3} - \dfrac{3}{11} =$ _____

8. $\dfrac{2}{3} - \dfrac{1}{6} =$ _____

9. $\dfrac{3}{4} - \dfrac{5}{8} =$ _____

10. $\dfrac{5}{12} - \dfrac{1}{8} =$ _____

Name _____   Date _____

Adding and Subtracting Fractions

Add the fractions and simplify.

1. $\dfrac{1}{2} + \dfrac{2}{5} =$

2. $\dfrac{2}{3} + \dfrac{2}{5} =$

3. $\dfrac{1}{5} + \dfrac{3}{4} =$

4. $\dfrac{1}{4} + \dfrac{5}{6} =$

5. $\dfrac{2}{5} + \dfrac{1}{2} + \dfrac{1}{10} =$

Subtract the fractions and simplify.

6. $\dfrac{5}{6} - \dfrac{1}{3} =$

7. $\dfrac{3}{4} - \dfrac{1}{3} =$

8. $\dfrac{2}{3} - \dfrac{5}{9} =$

9. $\dfrac{5}{7} - \dfrac{2}{3} =$

10. $\dfrac{3}{4} - \dfrac{2}{5} =$

ClayMaze.com

Fraction Multiplication

When multiplying or dividing fractions, the denominators do NOT need to be the same.

To multiply fractions, just multiply the numerators together and multiply the denominators together to find the product.

Example: Multiply the fractions.

a. $\dfrac{3}{5} \times \dfrac{1}{2} = \dfrac{3 \times 1}{5 \times 2} = \dfrac{3}{10}$

b. $\dfrac{1}{2} \times \dfrac{2}{3} \times \dfrac{3}{4} = \dfrac{1 \times 2 \times 3}{2 \times 3 \times 4} = \dfrac{6}{24} = \dfrac{1}{4}$

Tip on simplifying *(optional, but it can save time)*

See the 2's in the numerator and the denominator? Since both the numerator and the denominator only consist of products, those 2's can cancel each other out by division.

$$\dfrac{1 \times 2 \times 3}{2 \times 3 \times 4} \longrightarrow \dfrac{1 \times \cancel{2} \times 3}{\cancel{2} \times 3 \times 4}$$

The same is true for the 3's:

$$\dfrac{1 \times \cancel{2} \times \cancel{3}}{\cancel{2} \times \cancel{3} \times 4} \longrightarrow \dfrac{1}{4}$$

If, for example, there is a 2 in the numerator and 6 in the denominator, they can't cancel each other out completely, but they can still be reduced here, since 2 divides evenly into itself and 6. (2 ÷ 2 = 1 and 6 ÷ 2 = 3):

$$\dfrac{1}{6} \times \dfrac{2}{5} \times \dfrac{1}{3} = \dfrac{1 \times 2 \times 1}{6 \times 5 \times 3} = \dfrac{1 \times \overset{1}{\cancel{2}} \times 1}{\underset{3}{\cancel{6}} \times 5 \times 3} = \dfrac{1 \times 1 \times 1}{3 \times 5 \times 3} = \dfrac{1}{45}$$

Fraction Division

Before moving to fraction division, let's review some terminology:

Dividend, Divisor and Quotient
In a division problem, the **dividend** is the number being divided, the **divisor** is the number the dividend is divided by, and the **quotient** is the result of the division.

$$\text{dividend} \div \text{divisor} = \text{quotient}$$

Reciprocal
The **reciprocal** of a fraction is what you have when "flipping" the fraction by swapping the numerator and the denominator.

To **divide fractions**, multiply the dividend by the reciprocal of the divisor.

Example: Divide.

a. $\dfrac{4}{5} \div \dfrac{1}{3}$ $\xrightarrow{\text{dividend X reciprocal of divisor}}$ $\dfrac{4}{5} \times \dfrac{3}{1} = \dfrac{4 \times 3}{5 \times 1} = \dfrac{12}{5} = 2\dfrac{2}{5}$

b. $\dfrac{3}{4} \div 2$

2 can be rewritten as $\dfrac{2}{1}$ and the reciprocal of $\dfrac{2}{1}$ is $\dfrac{1}{2}$.

$\dfrac{3}{4} \div \dfrac{2}{1}$ $\xrightarrow{\text{dividend X reciprocal of divisor}}$ $\dfrac{3}{4} \times \dfrac{1}{2} = \dfrac{3 \times 1}{4 \times 2} = \dfrac{3}{8}$

c. $\dfrac{2}{8} \div \dfrac{5}{15}$ It's best to simplify the fractions first, so there are smaller numbers to work with.

$\dfrac{2}{8} \div \dfrac{5}{15}$ $\xrightarrow{\text{simplify}}$ $\dfrac{1}{4} \div \dfrac{1}{3}$ $\xrightarrow{\text{dividend X reciprocal of divisor}}$ $\dfrac{1}{4} \times \dfrac{3}{1} = \dfrac{3}{4}$

Name _____ Date _____

Multiplying and Dividing Fractions

Multiply the fractions and simplify.

1. $\dfrac{2}{5} \times \dfrac{1}{3} =$

2. $\dfrac{3}{8} \times \dfrac{1}{2} =$

3. $\dfrac{9}{10} \times \dfrac{1}{10} =$

4. $\dfrac{4}{7} \times \dfrac{3}{8} =$

5. $\dfrac{1}{2} \times \dfrac{2}{3} \times \dfrac{5}{8} =$

Divide the fractions and simplify.

6. $\dfrac{3}{4} \div \dfrac{1}{2} =$

7. $\dfrac{8}{11} \div 2 =$

8. $\dfrac{5}{9} \div \dfrac{2}{3} =$

9. $\dfrac{2}{3} \div \dfrac{1}{6} =$

10. $\dfrac{9}{10} \div \dfrac{2}{5} =$

ClayMaze.com

Name _____ Date _____

Multiplying and Dividing Fractions

Multiply the fractions and simplify.

1. $\dfrac{1}{6} \times \dfrac{4}{7} =$ _____

2. $\dfrac{2}{5} \times \dfrac{3}{4} =$ _____

3. $\dfrac{2}{4} \times \dfrac{1}{3} =$ _____

4. $\dfrac{2}{9} \times 3 =$ _____

5. $\dfrac{1}{3} \times \dfrac{5}{6} \times \dfrac{9}{10} =$ _____

Divide the fractions and simplify.

6. $\dfrac{3}{5} \div \dfrac{4}{9} =$ _____

7. $\dfrac{4}{7} \div \dfrac{2}{3} =$ _____

8. $\dfrac{1}{2} \div \dfrac{1}{4} =$ _____

9. $\dfrac{5}{8} \div \dfrac{2}{8} =$ _____

10. $\dfrac{6}{11} \div \dfrac{3}{7} =$ _____

ClayMaze.com

Decimals

5

Decimals and Place Value, Powers of 10, Converting Fractions and Decimals, Scientific Notation, Decimal Arithmetic, Percents

Decimals and Place Value

In the decimal part of a number, the farther away a digit is to the right of the decimal point, the smaller the value that digit has.

The first digit to the right of the decimal point is in the tenths place, the next is in the hundredths place, then the thousandths, then the ten thousandths, etc.

tenths ⌐ ⌐ hundredths

.2543

thousandths ⌐ ⌐ ten thousandths

2 tenths
5 hundredths
4 thousandths
3 ten thousandths

Example: Write the numbers in expanded form.

a. .7138   .7 + .01 + .003 + .0008

b. 23.059   20 + 3 + .05 + .009

Example: Sort the numbers from highest to lowest: .5, .007, .248, .03, .75, .25

To sort these, we need to compare the digits in the tenths place first, then hundredths, and then thousandths, since tenths > hundredths > thousandths.

The numbers with nonzero tenths place digits are .5, .248, .75 and .25. The highest tenths place digit for these is 7 followed by 5 and then 2. The first two numbers will be .75 and then .5.

Then we compare .248 and .25. Both have a 2 in the tenths place, but .25 is larger than .248 since its hundredths place digit is larger.

Next are .03 and .007. We only need to compare hundredths place digits to see that .03 > .007.

The ordered group of numbers from greatest to least is: .75, .5, .25, .248, .03, .007

Name _____   Date _____

Decimals

Write in expanded form.

1. 2.537 _____
2. 37.0215 _____
3. 418.0104 _____
4. 12.5239 _____
5. 53.674 _____

Evaluate.

1. _____   40 + 3 + .7 + .04 + .006
2. _____   200 + 1 + .8 + .05 + .0002
3. _____   9 + .7 + .004 + .0003 + .00001
4. _____   700 + 10 + 1 + .04 + .00003
5. _____   80 + 5 + .05 + .0002 + .00007

Order the numbers from least to greatest.

1. .462, .75, 1.1, .602, .09, .8 _____
2. .112, .099, 2.09, .873, 2.23, .41 _____
3. .056, 2.01, .094, .87, 2.005, .946 _____
4. .149, .322, .371, .192, .098, .243 _____
5. .15, 1.5, .085, .009, 1.28, .083 _____
6. .982, .003, .76, .984, .054, .0031 _____

Powers of 10

Powers of 10 are just as the name suggests: 10 raised to a power.

Positive powers of 10 (10 raised to a positive power) are numbers like the ones shown below:

$10^1 = 10$
$10^2 = 100$
$10^3 = 1{,}000$
$10^4 = 10{,}000$
$10^5 = 100{,}000$
...

Positive powers of ten have an **amount of 0's** equal to the power of the 10.

Negative powers of 10 (10 raised to a negative power) are numbers like the ones shown below:

$10^{-1} = .1$
$10^{-2} = .01$
$10^{-3} = .001$
$10^{-4} = .0001$
$10^{-5} = .00001$
...

Negative powers of ten have an **amount of decimal places** equal to the magnitude of the power of the 10.

The zeroth power of 10 is 1. $10^0 = 1$

Example: Evaluate.

a. 10^7

The exponent is 7, which is positive, so the number will be 1 followed by seven 0's.

_10,000,000_

b. 10^{-8}

The exponent is −8. It is negative and its magnitude is 8, so the number will have 8 decimal places with a 1 in the 8th decimal place.

_.00000001_

Example: Evaluate: $10^5 + 10^2 + 10^0 + 10^{-2} + 10^{-3}$

$10^5 + 10^2 + 10^0 + 10^{-2} + 10^{-3} = 100{,}000 + 100 + 1 + .01 + .001 =$ _100,101.011_

Name _____ Date _____

Powers of 10

Evaluate.

1. 10^8 _____
2. 10^{11} _____
3. 10^{-6} _____
4. 10^{-9} _____
5. 10^{12} _____

Write as powers of 10.

1. _____ 1,000,000
2. _____ .0000000001
3. _____ 1,000,000,000
4. _____ .0000001
5. _____ .000000000001

Evaluate.

1. $10^4 + 10^1 + 10^{-2} + 10^{-3}$ _____
2. $10^2 + 10^0 + 10^{-2} + 10^{-4}$ _____
3. $10^6 + 10^3 + 10^1 + 10^{-2}$ _____
4. $10^5 + 10^4 + 10^2 + 10^{-1}$ _____
5. $10^3 + 10^2 + 10^{-2} + 10^{-3} + 10^{-4}$ _____
6. $10^5 + 10^2 + 10^1 + 10^{-1} + 10^{-5}$ _____

ClayMaze.com

Converting Decimals and Fractions

Decimals to Fractions

Decimals can be represented by fractions as indicated by the name of the place value (tenths, hundredths, thousandths and so on).

Name	Decimal	Fraction
one tenth	.1	$\frac{1}{10}$
one hundredth	.01	$\frac{1}{100}$
one thousandth	.001	$\frac{1}{1,000}$

etc...

Example: Convert the decimal .003 to a fraction.

The 3 is in the thousandths place, so the fraction would be: $\frac{3}{1,000}$

Example: Convert the decimals to fractions.

a. .45

The denominator is determined by the farthest decimal place. In this case, 5 is in the farthest place, which is the **hundredths** decimal place. **100** will be the denominator.

The numerator will be the entire number past the decimal point starting with the first nonzero digit, which is 45.

This gives the fraction: $\frac{45}{100} \xrightarrow{\text{simplify}} \frac{9}{20}$

b. .028

The denominator is determined by the farthest decimal place. In this case, 8 is in the farthest place, which is the **thousandths** decimal place. **1,000** will be the denominator.

The numerator will be the entire number past the decimal point starting with the first nonzero digit, which is 28.

This gives the fraction: $\frac{28}{1,000} \xrightarrow{\text{simplify}} \frac{7}{250}$

Fractions to Decimals (Denominators That Are Powers of 10)

When converting a fraction with a power of 10 denominator, the result will be the numerator with its decimal point shifted to the left an amount of times equal to the number of 0's in the denominator.

To convert a fraction to a decimal when the denominator is a power of 10

1: Count the 0's in the denominator.

denominator: 10 ⟶ One 0: The decimal point will be shifted by 1.
denominator: 100 ⟶ Two 0's: The decimal point will be shifted by 2.
denominator: 1,000 ⟶ Three 0's: The decimal point will be shifted by 3.
and so on ...

2: Using the number in the numerator, shift the decimal point to the left by the amount determined in step 1, filling in empty decimal places with 0.

With integers, the decimal point is assumed to be at the end of the number. For example, 67 is the same as 67.0 (notice the decimal point after the 7).

Consider the fraction $\frac{71}{1,000}$.

A denominator of 1,000 is a power of 10 and has three 0's. This means that the decimal point in 71 will need to shift three places to the left.

The decimal point in 71 is right after the 1 (71 is the same as 71.0).
Shift its decimal point to the left by 3, filling in any empty decimal places with 0.

$\frac{71}{1,000}$ = .071   0 was filled in before the 7, since there was an empty decimal place.

Example: Find the decimals that represent the fractions.

a. $\frac{23}{100}$ 1. The denominator is a power of 10 and has **two** 0's.

   2. Shift the decimal point in 23 **two** places to the left: .23

b. $\frac{5}{1,000}$ 1. The denominator is a power of 10 and has **three** 0's.

   2. Shift the decimal point in 5 **three** places to the left, filling in any empty decimal places with 0:   .005

Name _____ Date _____

Converting Decimals and Fractions

Write the decimals as fractions and simplify.

1. .7 _____
2. .4 _____

3. .91 _____
4. .08 _____

5. .26 _____
6. .702 _____

7. .140 _____
8. .065 _____

9. .331 _____
10. .092 _____

Write the fractions as decimals.

11. $\dfrac{6}{10}$ _____
12. $\dfrac{21}{100}$ _____

13. $\dfrac{88}{100}$ _____
14. $\dfrac{64}{100}$ _____

15. $\dfrac{9}{10}$ _____
16. $\dfrac{5}{10}$ _____

17. $\dfrac{197}{1,000}$ _____
18. $\dfrac{852}{1,000}$ _____

19. $\dfrac{74}{100}$ _____
20. $\dfrac{37}{1,000}$ _____

21. $\dfrac{8}{10}$ _____
22. $\dfrac{2}{100}$ _____

23. $\dfrac{7}{1,000}$ _____
24. $\dfrac{722}{10,000}$ _____

Fractions to Decimals (Denominators That Are Not Powers of 10)

To convert a fraction to a decimal when the denominator is not a power of 10, try to find an equivalent fraction that does have a power of 10 denominator. Then convert it to a decimal using the method from the previous section.

Note: If an equivalent fraction with a power of 10 denominator is not apparent, then long division can be used (numerator ÷ denominator).

Example: Find the decimals that represent the fractions.

a. $\dfrac{3}{25}$

The first step is to find a power of 10 that 25 divides evenly into.
25 divides evenly into 100 (25x4 = 100), so we need an equivalent fraction with a denominator of 100.

$$\dfrac{3}{25} = \dfrac{?}{100}$$

Since 25 x 4 = 100, both the numerator and the denominator are multiplied by 4 to get the equivalent fraction with 100 as the denominator.

$$\dfrac{3}{25} = \dfrac{3(x4)}{25(x4)} = \dfrac{12}{100} = .12 \qquad \text{Shift the decimal point 2 places to the left in the 12.}$$

b. $\dfrac{1}{40}$

The first step is to find a power of 10 that 40 divides evenly into.
40 does not divide evenly into 100, but it does divide evenly into 1,000 (40x25 = 1,000). We need an equivalent fraction with a denominator of 1,000.

$$\dfrac{1}{40} = \dfrac{?}{1,000}$$

Since 40 x 25 = 1,000, both the numerator and the denominator are multiplied by 25 to get an equivalent fraction with a denominator of 1,000.

$$\dfrac{1}{40} = \dfrac{1(x25)}{40(x25)} = \dfrac{25}{1,000} = .025 \qquad \text{Shift the decimal point 3 places to the left in the 25, filling in any empty decimal places with 0.}$$

Name _____ Date _____

Converting Decimals and Fractions

Write the fractions as decimals.

1. $\dfrac{2}{5}$

2. $\dfrac{1}{20}$

3. $\dfrac{3}{8}$

4. $\dfrac{7}{25}$

5. $\dfrac{11}{40}$

6. $\dfrac{1}{2}$

7. $\dfrac{4}{25}$

8. $\dfrac{3}{4}$

9. $\dfrac{4}{5}$

10. $\dfrac{23}{50}$

Name _____ Date _____

Converting Decimals and Fractions

Write the fractions as decimals.

1. $\dfrac{1}{4}$

2. $\dfrac{3}{5}$

3. $\dfrac{6}{20}$

4. $\dfrac{2}{25}$

5. $\dfrac{1}{8}$

6. $\dfrac{23}{40}$

7. $\dfrac{10}{25}$

8. $\dfrac{9}{20}$

9. $\dfrac{3}{50}$

10. $\dfrac{2}{125}$

Multiplying by Powers of 10

When **multiplying by a power of ten with a positive exponent**, the decimal point is **shifted to the right** an amount of times equal to the power of the 10. The empty spaces are then filled by 0's.

Example: Multiply.

a. 41.532×10^2

 The exponent is 2, which is positive, so the decimal point will be shifted to the **right** 2 places.

 $41.532 \times 10^2 = 4153.2$

b. 237×10^4

 The exponent is 4, which is positive, so the decimal point will be shifted to the **right** 4 places, filling in 0's where needed.

 $237 \times 10^4 = 2370000. = 2,370,000$

When **multiplying by a power of ten with a negative exponent**, the decimal point is **shifted to the left** an amount of times equal to the magnitude of the power of the 10. The empty spaces are then filled by 0's.

Example: Multiply: 722.51×10^{-5}

 The exponent is -5, so the decimal point will be shifted to the **left** 5 places, filling in 0's where needed.

 $722.51 \times 10^{-5} = .0072251$

Name _____ Date _____

Multiplying by Powers of 10

Multiply.

1. $.42 \times 10^3$ _____
2. 2.1×10^{-2} _____

3. 8.811×10^1 _____
4. 142.8×10^4 _____

5. 2.44×10^2 _____
6. 208.3×10^1 _____

7. $.6452 \times 10^3$ _____
8. 79.05×10^{-3} _____

9. 131.5×10^{-2} _____
10. 122×10^5 _____

11. 17×10^{-5} _____
12. 80.39×10^{-4} _____

13. 5.5×10^{-3} _____
14. 38×10^1 _____

15. 143.7×10^0 _____
16. 1.071×10^{-5} _____

17. 0.41×10^2 _____
18. 16.22×10^{-2} _____

19. 203×10^{-3} _____
20. 14.3×10^5 _____

21. 15.1×10^{-1} _____
22. 145.5×10^3 _____

23. 72.7×10^5 _____
24. 58.15×10^{-1} _____

25. 8×10^{-4} _____
26. 5.68×10^2 _____

27. 41.9×10^4 _____
28. 13.8×10^{-2} _____

29. 53×10^1 _____
30. 6.21×10^0 _____

31. 78.2×10^3 _____
32. 170.4×10^4 _____

Scientific Notation

Scientific notation is a way to write a number in a specific format using a power of 10. This notation is often used to represent very large numbers or very small numbers, like the mass of the Earth (5.97×10^{24} kg) or the mass of a proton (1.673×10^{-27} kg).

In scientific notation, the value is represented by a number times 10 raised to a power. That number can be positive or negative, and its decimal point immediately follows the first digit.

Below are a few examples of numbers written in scientific notation:

Original Number	Scientific Notation
21,000,000	2.1×10^7
-324,500	-3.245×10^5
.0000000541	5.41×10^{-8}

Notice the number being multiplied by a power of 10 has only a single digit before the decimal point.

To change a number from scientific notation to a decimal or integer value, evaluate the expression using multiplication by a power of 10:

Shift the decimal point an amount of times equal to the magnitude of the power of the 10.
  If the power is positive, shift it to the right.
  If the power is negative, shift it to the left.

Example: Evaluate and express as decimal or integer values.

a. 7.32×10^{11}

   The power is 11, so the decimal point needs to be shifted to the **right** 11 places.

   $7.32 \times 10^{11} = 732{,}000{,}000{,}000$

b. 5×10^{-12}

   The power is −12. Since it is negative, the decimal point needs to be shifted to the **left** 12 places.

   $5 \times 10^{-12} = .000000000005$

To express a number in scientific notation:

First, write the number with the decimal point to the right of the first nonzero digit followed by any significant digits. This number will be multiplied by a power of 10.

The magnitude of the power is determined by how many places the decimal point needs to shift in order to equal the original number.

The sign of the power is determined by the direction the decimal point needs to shift. It will be positive if the decimal point needs to shift to the right or negative if it needs to shift to the left.

Example: Express the numbers in scientific notation.

a. .00527

The first nonzero digit is the 5. Place the decimal point after the 5 to get the first part.

$5.27 \times 10^?$

To figure out the 10's exponent, find how many places the decimal point needs to shift to get from the number part found in the first step (5.27) to the original number (.00527).

$5.27 \xrightarrow{\text{shift left 3 places}} .00527$

3 shifts to the left will turn 5.27 into .00527, so the magnitude of the exponent is 3. Since the decimal point needs to shift to the **left**, the exponent is **negative**.

$.00527 = 5.27 \times 10^{-3}$

b. 30,800,000

The first nonzero digit is the 3. Place the decimal point after the 3 to get the first part.

$3.08 \times 10^?$

To figure out the 10's exponent, find how many places the decimal point needs to shift to get from the number part found in the first step (3.08) to the original number (30,800,000).

$3.08 \xrightarrow{\text{shift right 7 places}} 30800000.$

7 shifts to the right will turn 3.08 into 30,800,000, so the magnitude of the exponent is 7. Since the decimal point needs to shift to the **right**, the exponent is **positive**.

$30,800,000 = 3.08 \times 10^7$

Name _____ Date _____

Scientific Notation

Evaluate and express as decimal or integer values.

1. 1.2×10^7 _____   2. 5.423×10^4 _____

3. 3.45×10^{-8} _____   4. 9.23×10^{-10} _____

5. 8×10^{-5} _____   6. 4.67×10^8 _____

7. 7.1×10^{11} _____   8. 2.86×10^{-6} _____

Write the numbers in scientific notation.

9. 515,000 _____   10. 72,600 _____

11. 340 _____   12. .106 _____

13. .0000000302 _____   14. .00691 _____

15. 72,000,000,000 _____   16. 52,020,000 _____

17. 290.3 _____   18. .00000176 _____

19. .00024 _____   20. 416,000 _____

21. 4,280,000,000 _____   22. .0258 _____

23. .000003684 _____   24. .000381 _____

25. .000045 _____   26. 318,000,000 _____

27. 4,100,000 _____   28. .0000506 _____

29. 56,100,000 _____   30. .012 _____

ClayMaze.com

Name _____ Date _____

Scientific Notation

Evaluate and express as decimal or integer values.

1. 3.511×10^5 _____   2. 8.5×10^{-4} _____

3. 7.1×10^{-7} _____   4. 2.23×10^2 _____

5. 1.40×10^{-4} _____   6. 5×10^8 _____

7. 4.3×10^{10} _____   8. 6.412×10^{-5} _____

Write the numbers in scientific notation.

9. 1,290,000 _____   10. .00000000822 _____

11. .0000495 _____   12. 771.1 _____

13. 483.4 _____   14. .00000059 _____

15. 6,100 _____   16. .0264 _____

17. 54,300,000 _____   18. 41,800,000,000 _____

19. .00000000091 _____   20. 34,000,000 _____

21. 8,306,000,000 _____   22. .0000002985 _____

23. 1,479 _____   24. .129 _____

25. 445,100 _____   26. 248,000 _____

27. 213.5 _____   28. .00043 _____

29. 8,120,000 _____   30. .000000000051 _____

ClayMaze.com

Decimal Addition and Subtraction

Adding and Subtracting Decimals

When adding or subtracting decimal numbers, it's very important to line them up so that their decimal points are in the same column. This way the digits of the same place value can be added or subtracted.

When lining up numbers in this way, 0's can be placed where applicable.

→ 0's can be appended to the **left** of the first digit of the **non-decimal** part of a number without changing its value.

> For example, 25 is the same as 025.

→ 0's can be appended to the **right** of the last digit of the **decimal part** of a number without changing its value.

> 4.57 is the same as 4.570 or even 4.5700000

Example: Add and Subtract.

a. 125.836 + 32.31

Rewrite the addition problem in column format, lining up the decimal points, then add the numbers.

```
        Decimal points are lined up.
   125.836
 + 032.310
 ---------
   158.146
```

b. 74 − 8.52

Rewrite the subtraction problem in column format, lining up the decimal points, then subtract the numbers.

74 does not have a visible decimal point, but 74 is the same as 74.00.

```
        Decimal points are lined up.
    74.00
  − 08.52
  -------
    65.48
```

Name _____   Date _____

Decimal Addition and Subtraction

Add and Subtract.

1. 8.17 + 52	2. .68 + 29.46	3. 16.9 − .63
4. .32 + 34.19	5. 52.25 − 12.4	6. 3.64 + 83.9
7. 43.5 − 42.73	8. 73.07 + .11	9. 48.4 − 47.64
10. 6.12 + 49.7	11. 70.9 − 42.81	12. 31.68 − 23.79
13. 28.95 − 28.7	14. 60.5 − 52.14	15. 71.97 + 8.9

64

ClayMaze.com

Decimal Multiplication

When multiplying with decimals you need to count the number of decimal places in both multipliers in order to place the decimal point in the product.

Step 1: Multiply the numbers as usual, ignoring the decimal points.

Step 2: Find the combined number of decimal places in both multipliers.

Step 3: Using the number of decimal places found in step 2, count back that many decimal places to the left in the product and place the decimal point.

Example: Multiply.

a. 1.5 x .4

Step 1: Multiply the numbers, ignoring decimal places for now: 15 x 4 = 60

Step 2: The number of decimal places in 1.5 is 1, and the number of decimal places in .4 is 1. The total number of decimal places is 1+1=2.

Step 3: Place the decimal point in the product by counting back 2 places (as determined in step 2).

.60   Placing the decimal point 2 places back gives .60 (or .6).

b. .102 x 3.4

Step 1: Multiply the numbers, ignoring decimal points for now.

```
    .102
  x 3.4
  -----
    408
   306
  -----
   3468
```
— Multiply ignoring decimal points.

Step 2: The number of decimal places in .102 is 3, and the number of decimal places in 3.4 is 1. The total number of decimal places is 3+1= 4.

Step 3: Place the decimal point in the product by counting back 4 places (as determined in step 2).

.3468   Placing the decimal point 4 places back gives .3468

Name _____ Date _____

Decimal Multiplication

Multiply.

1. .2 x .5 = _____
2. .7 x .9 = _____
3. .5 x .7 = _____
4. .3 x .5 = _____

5. 4 x .7 = _____
6. .9 x .3 = _____
7. .6 x 5 = _____
8. .2 x 8 = _____

9. .6 x 4 = _____
10. .8 x 6 = _____
11. .8 x 4 = _____
12. .1 x 7 = _____

13. 6.2
    x .5

14. 8 9
    x .4

15. 5 8
    x .4

16. 3 7
    x .8

17. 3 7
    x .2

18. 5 8
    x .9

19. 1.8
    x 7

20. 7 1
    x .5

21. 7 8
    x .9

22. 3.5
    x 9

23. 4.9
    x .5

24. 2.6
    x .2

25. 1 3 9
    x .7 4

26. 3.04
    x 8.6

27. 7.19
    x 5.2

28. 3 8.6
    x 2.2

29. 1.87
    x 3 2

30. 7 8.5
    x 6.5

66

ClayMaze.com

Decimal Division

When dividing decimal numbers, the divisor is changed into a non-decimal by multiplying by a power of 10, but the dividend must also be multiplied by the same power of 10.

Basically, the decimal point shifts to the right in both the divisor and dividend enough times so that the the divisor no longer has any decimal places.

→ *The amount of shifts in the divisor and the dividend needs to be the same.*

Example: Divide

a. $.7 \overline{) 5\,8.7\,3}$ Shift the decimal point **once** to the right in both the divisor and the dividend to get rid of any decimal places in the divisor.

$$.7 \xrightarrow{\text{shift right 1 place}} 7$$
$$58.73 \xrightarrow{\text{shift right 1 place}} 587.3$$

Now we can divide the numbers, placing the decimal point right above the new one in the dividend.

Decimal points are lined up.

```
       8 3.9
   7 ) 5 8 7.3
       5 6
         2 7
         2 1
           6 3
```

b. $.41 \overline{) 2.4\,1\,9}$ Shift the decimal point **twice** to the right in both the divisor and the dividend to get rid of any decimal places in the divisor.

$$.41 \xrightarrow{\text{shift right 2 places}} 41$$
$$2.419 \xrightarrow{\text{shift right 2 places}} 241.9$$

Now we can divide the numbers, placing the decimal point right above the new one in the dividend.

Decimal points are lined up.

```
         5.9
  4 1 ) 2 4 1.9
        2 0 5
          3 6 9
```

Name _____ Date _____

Decimal Division

Divide.

1. .9)16.65   2. .8)59.28   3. .3)20.04   4. .3)22.53

5. .8)63.76   6. .2)13.84   7. .8)328.8   8. .4)33.84

9. .3)15.75   10. .9)290.7   11. .2)10.88   12. .6)14.04

13. 2.6)88.92 14. .21)10.92 15. .37)22.57 16. 5.4)25.92

Percent

Percent indicates **how many parts out of 100**. It is written as a number followed by the percent sign (%), but can also be expressed as a decimal or a fraction.

Suppose there are **100** marbles in a bowl. 60 marbles are red and 40 marbles are blue.

Since there are 100 marbles and percent tells how many out of 100:

60% (60 percent) are red.
40% (40 percent) are blue.

Express Percent as a Decimal or a Fraction

As a decimal: Shift the decimal point of the number part two places to the left (since it is an amount out of 100).

As a fraction: Use the number part as the numerator with 100 as the denominator and simplify.

Example: Express as decimals and fractions.

a. 75%   To write 75% as a decimal, shift the decimal point two places to the left: .75

To write 75% as a fraction, use the number part (75) as the numerator with 100 as the denominator and simplify.

$$\frac{75}{100} = \frac{3}{4}$$

b. 5%   To write 5% as a decimal, shift the decimal point two places to the left: .05

To write 5% as a fraction, use the number part (5) as the numerator with 100 as the denominator and simplify.

$$\frac{5}{100} = \frac{1}{20}$$

When expressing a decimal as a percent, shift the decimal point two places to the right, then place the percent sign (%) after the number.

Example: Write the decimals as percents.

a. .12   Shift the decimal point two places to the right: 12%

b. .03   Shift the decimal point two places to the right: 3%

Finding a Quantity Given the Percentage (Calculating Percentages)

Step 1: Convert from percent to decimal.
Step 2: Multiply the decimal by the total amount of the whole.

*** When the whole amount is 100, the quantity of the part is the same as the number value of its percentage (since percent indicates how many out of 100).*

Suppose there is a box of 100 hats and 25% of those are blue. To find the amount of blue hats, convert from percent to decimal (.25) and multiply by the total amount of hats (100):

.25 x 100 = 25, so there are 25 blue hats.

Now suppose there are 80 total hats and 25% of those hats are blue. Follow the same method and convert from percent to decimal (.25), then multiply by the total amount of hats (80):

.25 x 80 = 20, so there are 20 blue hats.

Example: Calculate the percentages.

a. 43% of 100

Since the total amount is 100, 43% of the total is 43.

b. 20% of 60

Convert from percent to decimal (.2), then multiply by the whole (60):
.2 x 60 = 12

c. 42% of 75

Convert from percent to decimal (.42), then multiply by the whole (75):
.42 x 75 = 31.5

Example: Janice has a box of 30 marbles. If 50% of those marbles are blue, 30% are yellow and 20% are green, how many of each color does she have?

Convert from percent to decimal, then multiply by the whole amount:

Blue: .5 x 30 = 15   15 blue marbles

Yellow: .3 x 30 = 9   9 yellow marbles

Green: .2 x 30 = 6   6 green marbles

Name _____ Date _____

Percent

Write the percents as decimals.

1. 64% = _____　2. 5% = _____　3. 79% = _____　4. 10% = _____

5. 87% = _____　6. 38% = _____　7. 44% = _____　8. 2% = _____

9. 23% = _____　10. 20% = _____　11. 30% = _____　12. 16% = _____

Write the decimals as percents.

13. .01 = _____　14. .92 = _____　15. .5 = _____　16. .29 = _____

17. .25 = _____　18. .17 = _____　19. .08 = _____　20. .32 = _____

21. .74 = _____　22. .88 = _____　23. .31 = _____　24. .46 = _____

Calculate the percentages.

25. 63% of 52　26. 84% of 18　27. 32% of 90　28. 25% of 48

29. 4% of 55　30. 10% of 42　31. 88% of 87　32. 61% of 73

33. 23% of 21　34. 68% of 53　35. 21% of 92　36. 75% of 46

Name _____   Date _____

Percent

Word Problems

1. Cathy's clothing store normally sells t-shirts for $15. There is a sale for 12% off the regular t-shirt price. What is the cost of the t-shirts during the sale?

2. Mike and Jessica had lunch at a neighborhood restaurant that cost $42. What will be the total payment if they leave a 15% tip for the waiter?

3. Ten years ago, Erin bought a collectible game card for $5. The value of that card has increased by 75%. How much is it worth now?

4. James has a $20 gift card for a game. The game costs $19, but tax is 7%. Will the game card be enough to buy the game? What is the total cost of the game, including tax?

5. A local store is having a 20% off sale on shoes. If you want to buy a pair of shoes that normally sells for $75, and tax is 8%, how much will they cost in total? *(Calculate the tax amount **after** the discount is applied.)*

6. Expressions & Operations

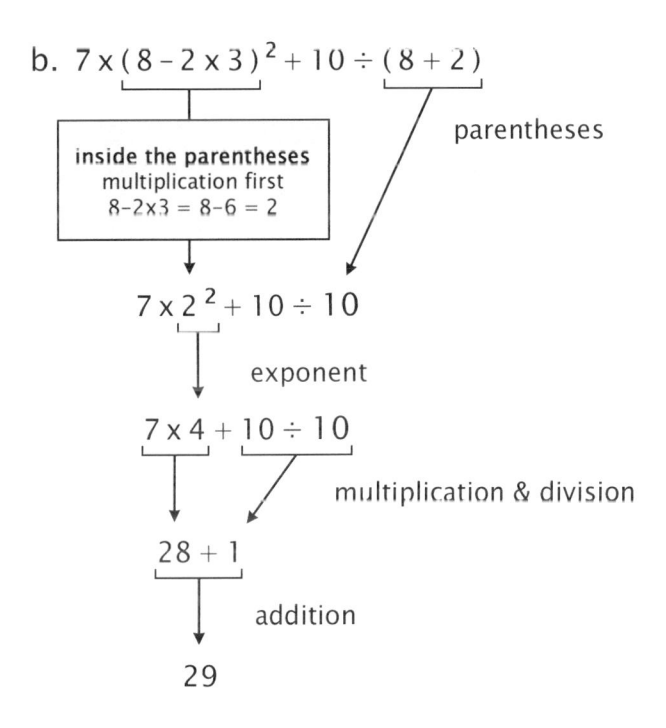

Order of Operations (PEMDAS), Expressions and Variables, Combining Like Terms, Substitution, Laws of Exponents, Expanding and Factoring Expressions

Order of Operations

In an expression like $3+5\times8$, the order in which the calculations are done matters, and we must follow the rules of the **order of operations** to obtain the correct answer.

This is the order in which operations need to be carried out in an expression:

1. **P**arentheses
2. **E**xponents
3. **M**ultiplication & **D**ivision (in the order they appear from left to right)
4. **A**ddition & **S**ubtraction (in the order they appear from left to right)

PEMDAS, the abbreviation for the phrase "Please Excuse My Dear Aunt Sally," can be used to help remember these rules.

Example: Evaluate $7\times(6-4)+10\div(2+8)$ and $7\times(8-2\times3)^2+10\div(8+2)$

a. $7\times(6-4)+10\div(2+8)$ — parentheses

$7\times2+10\div10$ — multiplication & division

$14+1$ — addition

15

b. $7\times(8-2\times3)^2+10\div(8+2)$ — parentheses

inside the parentheses multiplication first
$8-2\times3 = 8-6 = 2$

$7\times2^2+10\div10$ — exponent

$7\times4+10\div10$ — multiplication & division

$28+1$ — addition

29

73 — ClayMaze.com

Name _____ Date _____

Order of Operations (PEMDAS)

Evaluate.

1. $3 + 7 \times 5 - 2$

2. $7 + 15 \div (2 + 3) - 8$

3. $10 \times (3 + 4) - 8 \times 10 + 5$

4. $5 \div (2 \times 3 - 1) + 3 \times 11$

5. $7 + (2 \times 4 - 3)^2 \times 10$

6. $2 + (2 + 3 \times 4) \div (2 + 5) - 1$

7. $10 - 8 \times 2^2 \div 4 + 3 \times (8 - 6)$

8. $3 + 2 \times (3 + 1)^3 - (7 + 4)$

9. $3 \times (3 \times 5 - 4 \times 2) + (7 - 2 \times 3)^2$

10. $5 \times (9 - 4 \times 2 + 1)^4 + 10 \div (6 - 1)$

ClayMaze.com

Name _____ Date _____

Order of Operations (PEMDAS)

Evaluate.

1. $5 - 6 \div 2 + 8 \times 3$

2. $4 + 3 \times 7 - 10 \div 5$

3. $7 + (3 - 2 \times 2) + 8 \div 4$

4. $4 \times (3 + 5) - 6 \div 2 + 7 - 1$

5. $2 - (5 - 3) + 6 \times 2^2$

6. $3 - 4 \times 5 + (1 - 9)^2$

7. $4^2 - (2 - 3 \times 4)^2 + 10 \times 2 + 4$

8. $6 - 2 \times (3 + 1)^3 + (7 + 4)^2$

9. $3 \times (2 + 2 \times 3 + 1 \times 2)^0 + (1 - 2 \times 3)^2 - 3 \times 5$

10. $8 \times 2 + (12 \div 6)^2 - 7 \times 3^2 + (2 \times 2)^3$

Name _____ Date _____

Order of Operations (PEMDAS)

Evaluate.

1. $8 - 10 \div 5 + 7 \times 2$

2. $7 + 4 \times 7 - 12 \div 3$

3. $2 - 8 \times 2 + 10 + 20 \div 5$

4. $15 - (4 + 6 \times 3) \div 11 - 8$

5. $4 + (3 - 5 \times 2) \times (6 - 8) \div 7$

6. $(4 - 5 \times 2) \div (5 - 2^3) + 5 \times 2$

7. $10^2 - (6 \times 2 - 7)^2 + 5^2$

8. $12 + 3 \times (8 - 6)^3 - 4 \times (2 \times 3 - 1)^2$

9. $(16 - 20 \div 5 + 4) \div (2 \times 5 - 2^2 \times 3)^3$

10. $4 \times (7 - 6 \div 3 + 5) \div (5 + 8 \times 2 - 4 \times 5 + 1)^3$

76

ClayMaze.com

Expressions & Variables

Expressions can be used to represent amounts of things.

For example, if we know that a bag of marbles has 12 red marbles, 10 blue marbles and 5 green marbles, we can write the expression:

    12 + 10 + 5   to represent the total amount of marbles in the bag.

Letters are used to represent numbers when the value is unknown. These are called **variables**.

Using the example above, if we don't know how many green marbles there are, the letter x can be used to represent that amount:

    12 + 10 + x (where x represents the number of green marbles)

Example: Write an expression that represents 3 red balloons, an unknown amount of blue balloons, 1 purple balloon and 5 yellow balloons.

    __3 + x + 1 + 5__   The amount of blue balloons is unknown (represented by x).

When writing expressions with variables, it's best to not use the standard multiplication sign x, since x is a commonly used variable in expressions and will cause confusion.

In an expression using multiplication with a number and x, the number is placed next to the x.
    For example, 3 times x is written as 3x and 4 times y is written as 4y.

Parentheses can also be used to express multiplication: 3(x) is the same as 3x or 3 times x.

When using division in expressions, the division symbol is usually avoided as well, and is expressed using fractions.

    For example, (x + 3) ÷ 5x would be written as $\dfrac{x + 3}{5x}$.

Example: Write expressions for the descriptions.

  a. 5 times the number p   __5p__

  b. x squared minus 4   __$x^2 - 4$__

  c. 17 divided by the sum of 3 and m $\dfrac{17}{3+m}$

Example: The area of a rectangle is equal to its length times its width. The rectangle below has length x and width y, so its area would be x times y: area = xy.

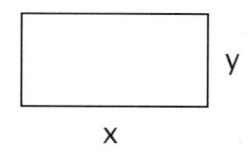

What is the area of a rectangle whose width is 2 units smaller then its length x?

length: x

width: x−2

area = x(x−2)

Example: A square is a type of rectangle, so its area is calculated the same way. However, because the lengths of its sides are equal, the area of a square whose sides are length s is s times s or s^2: area = s^2.

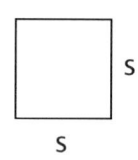

What is the area of a square whose sides are 4 units smaller than some number y?

side: y−4

area = (y−4)(y−4) = $(y-4)^2$

Example: The area of a triangle is equal to one half times its base times its height: area = $\frac{1}{2}$ bh.

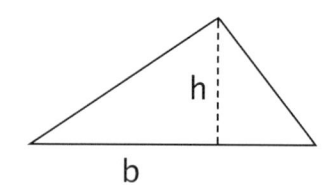

What is the area of a triangle whose base is twice the length of its height h?

base: 2h

height: h

area = $\frac{1}{2}$(2h)(h) = $\frac{1}{\cancel{2}}\cancel{2}$hh = h^2

Name _____   Date _____

Expressions & Variables

Write expressions for the descriptions below.

1. 21 decreased by x _____
2. 8 more than x _____
3. m increased by 35 _____
4. m divided by 20 _____
5. twice as many as p _____
6. y hundredths _____
7. 15 divided by y _____
8. the sum of 12 and q _____
9. x tenths _____
10. the product of 3 and v _____
11. y squared minus 3 _____
12. the square root of x _____
13. 2 fifths of m _____
14. 3 more than (x cubed) _____
15. 4 more than twice n _____
16. p fifths minus q _____
17. the cube root of v _____
18. z divided by (y cubed) _____
19. one half of the square root of the product of x and y _____
20. five times the sum of y cubed and 4 _____
21. the area of a rectangle whose length is five times its width w _____
22. the area of a square whose sides are 8 more than n _____
23. the area of a triangle whose base is 4 times its height h _____

Name _____ Date _____

Expressions & Variables

Write expressions for the descriptions below.

1. 100 more than s _____
2. 5 less than z _____

3. two fifths of x _____
4. p times q _____

5. x twentieths _____
6. m times the square of c _____

7. y squared plus 71 _____
8. f thirds _____

9. the sum of 20 and k _____
10. 8 more than (c times b) _____

11. z squared minus 45 _____
12. n plus y sixths _____

13. twice the sum of x and y _____
14. 3 divided by (x squared) _____

15. y thirds plus t sevenths _____
16. x squared minus 4 _____

17. x minus 7 plus 8 _____
18. 11 plus y eighths _____

19. the sum of the cubes of x, y and z _____

20. b squared minus the product of 4, a and c _____

21. the area of a rectangle whose length is twice its width w _____

22. the area of a square whose sides are 5 units less than t _____

23. the square root of the sum of n squared and m squared _____

Combining Like Terms

Terms, Variables, Coefficients and Constants
In an expression like the following:

$5x^2 + 3x + 2,$

the parts of the expression ($5x^2$, $3x$ and 2) are **terms**,
the letters representing numbers are **variables**,
the numbers multiplied by variables (5 and 3) are **coefficients** and
the stand-alone number (2) is a **constant**.

Example: Consider the expression $8x^3 - 4x^2 + x\ 2$.

a. List the terms. $\quad\underline{\quad 8x^3,\ -4x^2,\ x,\ -2 \quad}$

Notice that some of the terms are negative, because they are subtracted. The expression could even be rewritten like this:

$8x^3 + (-4x^2) + x + (-2)$

b. What is the coefficient of x^2? $\quad\underline{\quad -4 \quad}$

The term containing x^2 is $-4x^2$, so the coefficient is -4.

c. What is the coefficient of x? $\quad\underline{\quad 1 \quad}$

When a coefficient isn't visibly written next to the variable, it is considered 1. ($x = 1x$)

d. List any constants in the expression. $\quad\underline{\quad -2 \quad}$

Like Terms

In an expression, **like terms** are those that have the same variable(s) of the same power. These like terms can be combined by adding the coefficients (or subtracting if negative). The constants can be combined with other constants.

Below are some examples of like terms that are combined through addition and subtraction:

$3x - 11x = -8x$ Each term contains only x and its coefficient.

$4x^2 + 7x^2 = 11x^2$ Each term contains only x^2 and its coefficient.

Example: Simplify the expressions by combining like terms.

a. $4 + 2x - 8 + 3x + 10$

   Combine the like terms

   (1) Terms containing x: $2x$, $3x$

   $2x + 3x = 5x$

   (2) Constants: 4, −8, 10

   $4 - 8 + 10 = 6$

   Combine the expressions from (1) and (2):

   $\underline{5x + 6}$

b. $5x^2 + 21 + 7y - 4x - 2y - 4 + x - 3x^2$

   Combine the like terms

   (1) Terms containing x^2: $5x^2$, $-3x^2$

   $5x^2 - 3x^2 = 2x^2$

   (2) Terms containing x: $-4x$, x

   $-4x + x = -3x$

   (3) Terms containing y: $7y$, $-2y$

   $7y - 2y = 5y$

   (4) Constants: 21, −4

   $21 - 4 = 17$

   Combine the expressions from (1), (2), (3) and (4):

   $\underline{2x^2 - 3x + 5y + 17}$

Name _____ Date _____

Combining Like Terms

Rewrite the expressions by combining like terms.

1. $3x + 5 - 2x + 5$

2. $6y - 2 + 7y + 1$

3. $8x + 4 - 2x - 6 - x$

4. $x + 7 + 5x - 3 + x$

5. $7n^2 + n + 1 - 3n^2 - 4$

6. $5x^2 + x + 7 - 8x - 2x^2 - 2 + 3x$

7. $y^2 + 3y - 2 - 4y^2 - 2y + 5y^2 + 1$

8. $5x^4 + 3x^2 - 8y + 1 + 5y - 3x^4$

9. $x^3 + 5y^2 + 2x - 4x^3 - y^2 + 3$

10. $3n^2 - 5n - 4p - 2n^2 + 7p + 3$

11. $7y^4 + 3x^2 - x + 3 - y^4 + 5x^2 - 2x - 4x^2 - 2$

12. $4n^2 + .2n + 3m + 10 - 7m + 3n^2 + .8n - 8$

Name _____ Date _____

Combining Like Terms

Rewrite the expressions by combining like terms.

1. $4x + 7 - x - 3$

2. $6n - 2 + 7n + 8$

3. $10x - 3x + 5 - 2x + 1$

4. $4x + 1 - 2y - 5 + 3y$

5. $x^2 + 5 + 2x - 3 - 2x + 7$

6. $-3x^2 - 7x - 4y + x^2 + 8 + 3y$

7. $8m^2 + 4m - 2 - 5m^2 + 3 + 7m^2$

8. $4x^3 + 3x^2 - 8y + 6 + 9y - 2x^3 + 11$

9. $2x^2 - 2y^2 - z - 4 + 3x^2 + 3 - 2z$

10. $-4y^3 - 9x + 6z + 4y^3 + 1 - 4z + 5x$

11. $4x^3 - 2z^2 + 4x - y - 10 + 3z^2 + 9 - 4x - 6 - 8x^3$

12. $3x^2 + x + 7x - \frac{1}{5}y + 1 + 4x^2 + \frac{3}{5}y - x + 5$

Evaluating Expressions (Substitution)

In an expression with variables, if the value of a variable is known, the expression can be evaluated by **substituting** that value for the variable.

Example: Evaluate the following when $x = 4$ and $y = -1$.

a. $3x - 2 + y$ 4 is substituted for x and −1 is substituted for y:
$$3(4) - 2 + (-1) = 12 - 2 - 1 = 9$$

b. $2x(4x + 5)$

There are 2 things to note here:
1. Don't forget to follow the PEMDAS rules. Evaluate the expression in parentheses first.

2. Remember, using the multiplication symbol 'x' is avoided in these expressions, so any x's you see here are variables.

Use substitution with $x = 4$:

$$2x(4x + 5)$$

$$2(4)(4(4) + 5) = 8(16 + 5) = 8(21) = 168$$

c. $\dfrac{7 - x}{3x}$ 4 is substituted for x: $\dfrac{7 - 4}{3(4)} = \dfrac{3}{12} = \dfrac{1}{4}$

Substitution is useful when using formulas for things like finding areas and volumes or converting temperature in degrees Celcius to Fahrenheit.

Example: Evaluate.

a. What is the area of a triangle with height = 4 and base = 5? The formula for the area of a triangle is $\dfrac{1}{2}bh$, where b is the base and h is the height.

Substituting 5 for b and 4 for h: $\dfrac{1}{2}bh = \dfrac{1}{2}(5)(4) = \dfrac{20}{2} = 10$

b. Express 30°C in degrees Fahrenheit. The conversion formula is: $°F = °C\left(\dfrac{9}{5}\right) + 32$, where °F is the temperature in degrees Fahrenheit and °C is the temperature in degrees Celcius.

Substituting 30 for °C: $30\left(\dfrac{9}{5}\right) + 32 = 54 + 32 = 86 \,°F$

Name _____   Date _____

Evaluating Expressions (Substitution)

Evaluate the expressions with the given values.

1. $3x + 5$ if $x = 2$	2. $6x - 2$ if $x = -1$
3. $4x + 3y$ if $x=1, y=2$	4. $3p - 2q$ if $p = 2, q = -4$
5. $3s - 5 + 6t$ if $s=2, t = -2$	6. $2 + 4x - 7y$ if $x = -1, y = 5$
7. $5x(2x - 4y)$ if $x = 4, y = -3$	8. $2(a^2 + b^2)$ if $a = -4, b = 6$
9. $\dfrac{4y - 5}{2y - x + z}$ if $x = -1, y = 5, z = 4$	10. $\dfrac{2z(4m - 1)^2}{m - 4}$ if $n = 6, m = 3, z = -1$

Express the temperatures below in degrees Fahrenheit using the conversion formula. Use substitution to find the answers.

The conversion formula is: $°F = °C\left(\dfrac{9}{5}\right) + 32$

11. $10°C = $ _____ $°F$ 12. $30°C = $ _____ $°F$

Rules of Exponents

When dealing with expressions involving exponents, some rules and definitions can help greatly in simplifying and manipulating expressions.

For some number x, if m and n are integers {..., -2, -1, 0, 1, 2, ...},

Zero Exponent:

(1) $x^0 = 1$

Negative Exponent:

(2) $x^{-n} = \dfrac{1}{x^n}$ if $x \neq 0$

Multiplying Powers of the Same Base:

(3) $x^m x^n = x^{m+n}$

Dividing Powers of the Same Base:

(4) $\dfrac{x^m}{x^n} = x^{m-n}$ if $x \neq 0$

Power of a Power:

(5) $(x^m)^n = x^{mn}$

The trick to solving problems using the power rules is to find the one that matches the format of the expression you're dealing with. Remember that x, m and n just represent numbers.

Example: Evaluate the following.

a. $\dfrac{8^{12}}{8^{10}}$ Since 8^{12} and 8^{10} are very large numbers, this calculation could be very tedious. However, the expression fits the format of rule (4) above, which can be used to make this much easier to evaluate.

Rule (4): $\dfrac{x^m}{x^n} = x^{m-n}$ $\dfrac{8^{12}}{8^{10}} = 8^{12-10} = 8^2 = 64$

b. $5^{-8} 5^6$ This one will be much easier after it's simplified by using the rules. The expression matches the format of rule (3), so we'll use that first.

Rule (3): $x^m x^n = x^{m+n}$ $5^{-8} 5^6 = 5^{-8+6} = 5^{-2}$

Now, let's get rid of the negative exponent using rule (2).

Rule (2): $x^{-n} = \dfrac{1}{x^n}$ $5^{-2} = \dfrac{1}{5^2} = \dfrac{1}{25}$

Example: Rewrite the following expressions using the rules of exponents and express with no negative exponents.

For these problems, look at each expression and use the closest matching format in the rules on the previous page to simplify them.

a. $x^4 x^2$ This expression is the product of powers of the same base, so rule (3) is the closest match.

    Using rule (3): $x^m x^n = x^{m+n}$

$$x^4 x^2 = x^{4+2} = x^6$$

b. $y^4 y^{-7}$ This expression is the product of powers of the same base, so rule (3) is the closest match.

    Using rule (3): $x^m x^n = x^{m+n}$

$$y^4 y^{-7} = y^{4+(-7)} = y^{4-7} = y^{-3}$$

Next, the negative exponent should be changed to positive, so rule (2) is used.

    Using rule (2): $x^{-n} = \dfrac{1}{x^n}$

$$y^{-3} = \dfrac{1}{y^3}$$

c. $\dfrac{b^4}{b^3}$ This expression is the quotient of powers of the same base, so rule (4) is the closest match.

    Using rule (4): $\dfrac{x^m}{x^n} = x^{m-n}$

$$\dfrac{b^4}{b^3} = b^{4-3} = b^1 = b$$

d. $(z^2)^5$ This expression is the power of a power, so rule (5) is the closest match.

    Using rule (5): $(x^m)^n = x^{mn}$

$$(z^2)^5 = z^{(2)(5)} = z^{10}$$

Name _____ Date _____

Rules of Exponents

Evaluate the expressions. (Use the rules of exponents to help simplify them first.)

1. $7^{10}7^{-8} =$

2. $3^{-7}3^{4} =$

3. $\dfrac{4^{8}}{4^{5}} =$

4. $2^{-56}2^{61} =$

5. $(2^{2})^{4} =$

6. $\dfrac{(-5)^{15}}{(-5)^{12}} =$

Rewrite the expressions using the rules of exponents and express without parentheses or negative exponents. Remember: $x^{-n} = \dfrac{1}{x^{n}}$ and $x^{n} = \dfrac{1}{x^{-n}}$

7. $x^{4}x^{3}$

8. $n^{12}n^{-8}$

9. $y^{3}y^{-8}$

10. $x^{2}x^{5}x^{4}$

11. $\dfrac{z^{4}}{z^{-4}}$

12. $\dfrac{x^{20}}{x^{15}}$

13. $\dfrac{b^{-3}b^{8}}{b^{2}}$

14. $(s^{3})^{5}$

15. $(x^{2})^{-4}$

16. $\dfrac{y(y^{4})^{3}}{y^{8}}$

Name _____ Date _____

Rules of Exponents

Evaluate the expressions. (Use the rules of exponents to help simplify them first.)

1. $2^3 2^2 =$

2. $3^8 3^{-4} =$

3. $(10^3)^2 =$

4. $\dfrac{11^{22}}{11^{23}} =$

5. $4^{-15} 4^{12} =$

6. $\dfrac{(278^{32})(278^{-22})}{278^{10}} =$

Rewrite the expressions using the rules of exponents and express without parentheses or negative exponents. Remember: $x^{-n} = \dfrac{1}{x^n}$ and $x^n = \dfrac{1}{x^{-n}}$

7. $y^{-2} y^8$

8. $x^9 x^7$

9. $\dfrac{b^{10}}{b^3}$

10. $x^n x^{-n}$

11. $z^5 z^{-4} z^3$

12. $\dfrac{b^{-2}}{b^{-3}}$

13. $\dfrac{c^8}{c^4 c^{-7}}$

14. $x^{2n} x^n$

15. $(n^5)^{-2}$

16. $\left(\dfrac{1}{y^{-3}}\right)^4$

Rules of Exponents (continued)

The previous section covered some rules of exponents for dealing with only one number or variable as the base. Below are the same rules with two more added.

These two new rules, (6) and (7), are for expressions involving more than one number or variable. Notice the different variables: x and y, as opposed to just x.

For numbers x and y, if m and n are integers {..., -2, -1, 0, 1, 2, ...},

Zero Exponent:

(1) $x^0 = 1$

Negative Exponent:

(2) $x^{-n} = \dfrac{1}{x^n}$ if $x \neq 0$

Multiplying Powers of the Same Base:

(3) $x^m x^n = x^{m+n}$

Dividing Powers of the Same Base:

(4) $\dfrac{x^m}{x^n} = x^{m-n}$ if $x \neq 0$

Power of a Power:

(5) $(x^m)^n = x^{mn}$

Power of a Product:

(6) $(xy)^n = x^n y^n$

Power of a Quotient:

(7) $\left(\dfrac{x}{y}\right)^n = \dfrac{x^n}{y^n}$ if $y \neq 0$

Example: Rewrite the following expressions using the rules of exponents.

a. $(xy)^3$ Rule (6) is the closest match for this expression.

Using rule (6): $(xy)^n = x^n y^n$

$(xy)^3 = x^3 y^3$

b. $\left(\dfrac{r}{s}\right)^4$ Rule (7) is the closest match for this expression.

Using rule (7): $\left(\dfrac{x}{y}\right)^n = \dfrac{x^n}{y^n}$

$\left(\dfrac{r}{s}\right)^4 = \dfrac{r^4}{s^4}$

Example: Rewrite the following expressions using the rules of exponents and express with no negative exponents.

a. $(4n)^2$ This expression is the power of a product of 2 different numbers (4 and n), so rule (6) is the closest match.

Using rule (6): $(xy)^n = x^n y^n$

$$(4n)^2 = 4^2 n^2 = 16n^2$$

b. $(7x^3)^2$ This one may look a little more complex because of the x^3, but that x^3 just represents a number. So the expression $(7x^3)^2$ can be treated as the power of a product of two numbers (7 and x^3). Rule (6) is the closest match.

Using rule (6): $(xy)^n = x^n y^n$

$$(7x^3)^2 = 7^2 (x^3)^2$$

Rule (5) can be used on part of the expression: $(x^3)^2$

Using rule (5): $(x^m)^n = x^{mn}$

$$7^2 (x^3)^2 = 49 x^{(3)(2)} = 49 x^6$$

c. $\left(\dfrac{r^3}{t^4}\right)^2$ Just like the problem above, we can treat the expressions r^3 and t^4 as just two different numbers. Then the whole expression is just a power of the quotient of two numbers (r^3 and t^4). Rule (7) is the closest match.

Using rule (7): $\left(\dfrac{x}{y}\right)^n = \dfrac{x^n}{y^n}$

$$\left(\dfrac{r^3}{t^4}\right)^2 = \dfrac{(r^3)^2}{(t^4)^2}$$

Rule (5) can be used on both parts of the expression: $(r^3)^2$ and $(t^4)^2$

Using rule (5): $(x^m)^n = x^{mn}$

$$\dfrac{(r^3)^2}{(t^4)^2} = \dfrac{r^{(3)(2)}}{t^{(4)(2)}} = \dfrac{r^6}{t^8}$$

Name _____   Date _____

Rules of Exponents

Rewrite the expressions using the rules of exponents and express with no parentheses or negative exponents. *Hint: When possible, simplify complex expressions inside parentheses first.*

1. $(xy)^8$

2. $(2y)^3$

3. $\left(\dfrac{n}{m}\right)^4$

4. $\left(\dfrac{10}{s}\right)^2$

5. $(6x^4)^2$

6. $\left(\dfrac{n^2}{m}\right)^3$

7. $\left(\dfrac{2}{x^{-2}}\right)^3$

8. $(x^2y^3)^4$

9. $\left(\dfrac{n^4 m^2}{5m}\right)^3$

10. $\left(\dfrac{x^3 y}{xy^2}\right)^2$

11. $\left(\dfrac{c^4}{b^2}\right)^{-3}$

12. $\left(\dfrac{n^{-2}}{m^{-4}}\right)^{-1}$

Name _____   Date _____

Rules of Exponents

Rewrite the expressions using the rules of exponents and express with no parentheses or negative exponents. *Hint: When possible, simplify complex expressions inside parentheses first.*

1. $(xn^2)^4$

2. $\left(\dfrac{y}{t^3}\right)^3$

3. $\left(\dfrac{t^2}{5}\right)^3$

4. $(s^{-2}r^3)^2$

5. $\dfrac{(10n^{-4})^2}{100}$

6. $\left(\dfrac{r^7}{s^{-4}}\right)^0$

7. $\left(\dfrac{n^3}{m^2}\right)^{-4}$

8. $\left(\dfrac{4p^2}{m^5}\right)^3$

9. $(3x^2y^{-3})^{-2}$

10. $\left(\dfrac{b(b^4)}{c^3}\right)^2$

11. $\left(\dfrac{n^4m^{-2}}{m^3n^2}\right)^2$

12. $\left(\dfrac{2x^{-2}y}{y^2x^3}\right)^{-3}$

Distributive Property

The distributive property is used to "expand" expressions when a number is multiplied by the sum (or difference) of numbers.

Distributive Property

If a, b and c are real numbers,

a(b+c) = ab + ac

This also works with subtraction:

a(b-c) = ab - ac

The multiplier outside of the parentheses, represented by a, is multiplied by each term inside of the parentheses.

Note: It's very important to keep track of signs when using the distributive property!

Example: Expand the expressions using the distributive property.

a. $2(x + 3) = 2x + 2(3)$
$= 2x + 6$

b. $4(x - 5) = 4x - 4(5)$
$= 4x - 20$

c. $5(x^2 + 7) = 5x^2 + 5(7)$
$= 5x^2 + 35$

The distributive property can be used when there are more than two terms inside of the parentheses. The multiplier is multiplied by each term (paying attention to the signs + and -).

a(b + c + d) = ab + ac + ad

a(b - c - d) = ab - ac - ad

Example: Expand the expressions using the distributive property.

a. $3(x + y + 4) = 3x + 3y + 3(4)$
$= 3x + 3y + 12$

b. $2(x^2 + 6x - 8) = 2x^2 + 2(6x) - 2(8)$
$= 2x^2 + 12x - 16$

c. $7(x^2 - 2y + 5) = 7x^2 - 7(2y) + 7(5)$
$= 7x^2 - 14y + 35$

These can get a little more complex and the multiplier can be an expression containing variables. With these, you may need to use the rules of exponents.

Example: Expand the expressions using the distributive property.
(Remember to pay attention to signs.)

a. $4x(2x - 3) = 4x(2x) - 4x(3)$
$= 8x^2 - 12x$

b. $-3y(y - 2z - 1) = -3y(y) - (-3y)(2z) - (-3y)(1)$
$= -3y^2 + 6yz + 3y$

c. $2x^2(x^3 + 3x^2 + 2) = 2x^2(x^3) + 2x^2(3x^2) + 2x^2(2)$
$= 2x^{2+3} + 6x^{2+2} + 4x^2$
$= 2x^5 + 6x^4 + 4x^2$

d. $5xy(x^2 - 4y + 7z - 2) = 5xy(x^2) - 5xy(4y) + 5xy(7z) - 5xy(2)$
$= 5x^{1+2}y - 20xy^{1+1} + 35xyz - 10xy$
$= 5x^3y - 20xy^2 + 35xyz - 10xy$

Name _____   Date _____

Distributive Property

Use the distributive property to expand the expressions.

1. $2(x + 5)$

2. $5(x - 3)$

3. $4(y + 10)$

4. $x(x + 3)$

5. $x(-x + 7)$

6. $2x(x + 5)$

7. $2n(n + 10)$

8. $2x(x^2 - 1)$

9. $3x(6x^2 - 8x)$

10. $-n(n^2 + n - 11)$

11. $5x(2x^2 + 3x - 1)$

12. $x(4x^2 - 3x - 2y)$

13. $xy(4x^2 - 3xy + y^2)$

14. $x^2(2x^2 - 3y - 4xy)$

Name _____ Date _____

Distributive Property

Use the distributive property to expand the expressions.

1. $5(n + 2)$

2. $2(x - 4)$

3. $3(z - 8)$

4. $x(x - 1)$

5. $-3y(y + 2)$

6. $2x(x - 4)$

7. $5x(x - 5)$

8. $-3(-x^2 - 2)$

9. $4x(2x^2 + 3)$

10. $2x(10x^2 + 7y)$

11. $-7x(2x^2 - 3x + 5)$

12. $-x(2x^3 - 3x^2 + 4)$

13. $xy(2x^2 + 3xy + 2y)$

14. $xy^2(-x^2y + 7xy^2 - 2y + 8)$

Distributing / Expanding (continued)

Sometimes both multipliers have more than one term and may look something like this:
(a + b)(c + d)

To expand an expression like this, all that needs to be done is to multiply each term in the first set of parentheses by each term in the second set of parentheses.

a is distributed to (c + d) and then b is also distributed to (c + d):

1. Multiply the first term (a) by each term in the second parentheses (c and d):
   a(c + d) = ac + ad

2. Multiply the second term (b) by each term in the second parentheses (c and d):
   b(c + d) = bc + bd

Combine the two expressions from steps 1 and 2:
(a + b)(c + d) = ac + ad + bc + bd

Example: Expand the expression and combine like terms:

(x + 2)(x + 5)

Following the steps above, each term of the first expression in parentheses is distributed to each term of the second expression in parentheses.

Step 1: Multiply the first term in (x + 2), which is **x**, by (x + 5)

Step 2: Multiply the second term in (x + 2), which is **2**, by (x + 5)

(x + 2)(x + 5) = x(x + 5) + 2(x + 5)
                  ‾‾‾‾‾‾‾‾   ‾‾‾‾‾‾‾‾
                   Step 1   Step 2

= x(x) + x(5) + 2x + 2(5)
  ‾‾‾‾‾‾‾‾‾‾‾   ‾‾‾‾‾‾‾‾‾
    Step 1   Step 2
   expanded   expanded

= x^2 + 5x + 2x + 10   *Combine like terms: 2x + 5x = 7x*

= x^2 + 7x + 10

Example: Expand the expression and combine like terms:

$(x - 2)(x + 4)$

> Each term of the first expression in parentheses is distributed to each term of the second expression in parentheses.
>
> **Step 1:** Multiply the first term in $(x - 2)$, which is **x**, by $(x + 4)$
>
> **Step 2:** Multiply the second term in $(x - 2)$, which is **−2**, by $(x + 4)$
>
> $(x - 2)(x + 4) = \underbrace{x(x + 4)}_{\text{Step 1}} \underbrace{- 2(x + 4)}_{\text{Step 2}}$
>
> $= \underbrace{x(x) + x(4)}_{\substack{\text{Step 1} \\ \text{expanded}}} \underbrace{- 2(x) - 2(4)}_{\substack{\text{Step 2} \\ \text{expanded}}}$
>
> $= x^2 + 4x - 2x - 8$
>
> $= x^2 + 2x - 8$

When there are more than two terms in the parentheses, the same idea applies:

Multiply each term in the first set of parentheses by each term in the second set of parentheses.

Example: Expand the expression and combine like terms:

$(x - 3)(x^2 + 2x - 1)$

> Each term of the first expression in parentheses is distributed to each term of the second expression in parentheses.
>
> **Step 1:** Multiply the first term in $(x - 3)$, which is **x**, by $(x^2 + 2x - 1)$
>
> **Step 2:** Multiply the second term in $(x - 3)$, which is **−3**, by $(x^2 + 2x - 1)$
>
> $(x - 3)(x^2 + 2x - 1) = \underbrace{x(x^2 + 2x - 1)}_{\text{Step 1}} \underbrace{- 3(x^2 + 2x - 1)}_{\text{Step 2}}$
>
> $= \underbrace{x(x^2) + x(2x) - x(1)}_{\text{Step 1 expanded}} \underbrace{- 3(x^2) - 3(2x) - 3(-1)}_{\text{Step 2 expanded}}$
>
> $= x^3 + 2x^2 - x - 3x^2 - 6x + 3$
>
> $= x^3 - x^2 - 7x + 3$

Name _____ Date _____

Distributing / Expanding

Expand the expressions and combine like terms.

1. (x + 1)(x + 2)

2. (x + 3)(x + 4)

3. (x − 1)(x + 5)

4. (x − 2)(x + 2)

5. (x + 4)(x − 3)

6. (x + 5)(x + 5)

7. (x + 1)(x² + 1)

8. (x + 2)(x² − x)

9. (x + 2)(x² + 2x + 3)

10. (x − 4)(x² + 3x − 2)

Name _____ Date _____

Distributing / Expanding

Expand the expressions and combine like terms.

1. $(x - 4)(x + 5)$

2. $(x - 10)(x + 5)$

3. $(x + 1)(x - 1)$

4. $(n + 3)(3n + 1)$

5. $(4y + 5)(y - 1)$

6. $(2x - 1)(x + 3)$

7. $(3x + 2)(-x + 4)$

8. $(n^2 + 2)(n^2 - 4)$

9. $(x + 3)(x^2 + 5x - 2)$

10. $(x - 5)(2x^2 - x + 1)$

Factoring Expressions

Factoring an expression is basically the opposite of distributing.

The distributive property is used to expand an expression:

$2x(x + 4) \longrightarrow 2x^2 + 8x$

However, factoring is the reverse of expanding (opposite of the above):

$2x^2 + 8x \longrightarrow 2x(x + 4)$.

To do this, you'll need to find two factors and then write them as a product.

Step 1: Find the first factor.
   (a) Find the GCF of the numbers (constants and coefficients).
   (b) If all terms have a common variable, find the smallest power of that variable; otherwise, skip this step.
   (c) Multiply the result found in (a) by the result found in (b).
   If no common variable was found in (b), then the first factor is just the GCF from (a).

Step 2: Find the second factor.
   Divide the original expression by the first factor by dividing each term by that factor.

Step 3: Write as a product.
   The result is written as the product of the first factor and the second factor.

Example: Factor the expression $3x + 6$

Step 1: Find the first factor.
   (a) The numbers in the terms are 3 and 6. The GCF of 3 and 6 is 3.
   (b) Only one term has a variable, so that can't be factored out.
   (c) Since there are no common variables, the first factor is just the GCF found in (a):   3

Step 2: Find the second factor.
   Divide the original expression ($3x + 6$) by the factor found in Step 1 by dividing each term by that factor:

   $$\frac{3x + 6}{3} = \frac{3x}{3} + \frac{6}{3} = x + 2 \qquad (3/3 = 1 \text{ and } 6/3 = 2)$$

Step 3: The result is written as the product of the first factor (3) and the second factor ($x + 2$):

   $3(x + 2)$

Example: Factor the expression: $4x^3 + 6x^2$

Step 1: Find the first factor.
 (a) The coefficients in the terms are 4 and 6. The GCF of 4 and 6 is 2.
 (b) The common variable in the terms of the expression is x, and the smallest power is x^2.
 (c) Multiply the results found in (a) and (b): $2x^2$

Step 2: Find the second factor.
Divide the original expression ($4x^3 + 6x^2$) by the factor found in Step 1 by dividing each term by that factor:

$$\frac{4x^3 + 6x^2}{2x^2} = \frac{4x^3}{2x^2} + \frac{6x^2}{2x^2} = 2x^{3-2} + 3x^{2-2} = 2x^1 + 3x^0 = 2x + 3$$

Step 3: The result is the product of the first factor ($2x^2$) and the second factor ($2x + 3$):
 $2x^2(2x + 3)$

This same method can be used for expressions with more than one variable.

Example: Factor the expression: $3x^4y^2 + 15x^3y$

Step 1: Find the first factor.
 (a) The coefficients are 3 and 15. The GCF of 3 and 15 is 3.
 (b) The common variables in both terms of the expression are x and y, and the smallest powers are x^3 and y^1. x^3y
 (c) Multiply the results found in (a) and (b): $3x^3y$

Step 2: Find the second factor.
Divide the original expression ($3x^4y^2 + 15x^3y$) by the factor found in Step 1 by dividing each term by that factor:

$$\frac{3x^4y^2 + 15x^3y}{3x^3y} = \frac{3x^4y^2}{3x^3y} + \frac{15x^3y}{3x^3y}$$

$$= x^{4-3}y^{2-1} + 5x^{3-3}y^{1-1} = x^1y^1 + 5x^0y^0 = xy + 5$$

Step 3: The result is the product of the first factor ($3x^3y$) and the second factor ($xy + 5$):
 $3x^3y(xy + 5)$

Name _____ Date _____

Factoring Expressions

Factor the expressions.

1. $4x + 2$

2. $2x - 16$

3. $5x - 15$

4. $3y + 9$

5. $6n^2 + 24n$

6. $8x^2 - 40x$

7. $12x^2 + 16x$

8. $4x^2 + 20x$

9. $5x^4y^3 + 10x^5y^2$

10. $2n^4m^3 + 8n^3m^2$

Name _____   Date _____

Factoring Expressions

Factor the expressions.

1. $2x + 8$

2. $5x - 10$

3. $3n - 21$

4. $6x^2 + 10x$

5. $4x^2 + 16x$

6. $3c^2 - 15c$

7. $2x^3 - 7x^2$

8. $12x^4 + 15x^3$

9. $2x^2y^2 + 4xy$

10. $3x^3y + 6x^2y^2$

Equations

One-Step Equations, Two-Step Equations, Combining Like Terms to Solve Equations

One-Step Equations

An **equation** is a statement showing that the expressions on each side of the equal sign have the same value.

The focus of solving equations is to isolate the variable to one side of the equal sign to find its value. Mathematical operations like addition, subtraction, multiplication and division can be used to accomplish this.

Remember when solving equations:
Whatever is done to one side of the equal sign must be done to the other side.
 If a quantity is added, subtracted, multiplied or divided on one side of the equal sign, that same operation needs to happen on the other side in order to keep both sides equal.

One-step equations require only one mathematical operation, done on both sides of the equal sign to isolate the variable.

Example: Solve the equation by finding the value of the variable x.

$x + 5 = 10$

 The goal is to isolate the variable x to one side of the equal sign. This can be done by getting the $+5$ away from the x.

  In order to get rid of the $+5$, we can subtract 5, but this must be done on BOTH sides of the equal sign.

$$x + 5 = 10$$
$$\downarrow$$
$$x + 5 - 5 = 10 - 5 \qquad \textit{Subtract 5 from both sides to isolate the variable. } (5-5=0)$$
$$\downarrow$$
$$x = 5$$

Example: Solve the equation by finding the value of the variable y.

$28 = y - 2$

Isolate the variable (get rid of the − 2 near the variable y) by adding 2 to **BOTH** sides of the equal sign.

$28 = y - 2$

$28 + 2 = y - 2 + 2$ *Add 2 to both sides. (−2+2=0)*

$30 = y$ or $y = 30$

Example: Solve the equations by finding the value of the variable x.

a. $\dfrac{x}{4} = 20$ Since x is **divided** by 4, multiplication by 4 is used to cancel out the 4 in the denominator (4/4=1).

Isolate the variable by multiplying **BOTH** sides by 4.

$\dfrac{x}{4} = 20$

$\dfrac{(4)x}{4} = 20(4)$ *Multiply both sides by 4. (The 4's cancel out: 4/4 = 1)*

$1x = 80$

$x = 80$

b. $3x = 15$

Isolate the variable by dividing **BOTH** sides by 3.

$3x = 15$

$\dfrac{3x}{3} = \dfrac{15}{3}$ *Divide both sides by 3. (The 3's cancel out: 3/3 = 1)*

$1x = 5$

$x = 5$

Name _____ Date _____

One-Step Equations

Solve for x.

1. $x + 4 = 20$	2. $4x = 12$	3. $x + 22 = 55$
4. $x - 12 = 37$	5. $3x = 48$	6. $-8x = 120$
7. $\dfrac{x}{5} = 20$	8. $12x = 8$	9. $\dfrac{x}{2} = 15$
10. $x - 3 = -48$	11. $\dfrac{x}{3} = -21$	12. $3x = -150$
13. $\dfrac{x}{7} = -34$	14. $-41 + x = 67$	15. $\dfrac{x}{4} = \dfrac{1}{2}$

ClayMaze.com

Name _____ Date _____

One-Step Equations

Solve for x.

1. $3x = 2$

2. $x + 27 = 10$

3. $15x = 3$

4. $\dfrac{x}{10} = -20$

5. $17x = 51$

6. $\dfrac{x}{7} = -44$

7. $32 + x = -30$

8. $\dfrac{x}{5} = 45$

9. $x - 29 = 16$

10. $x - 14 = 57$

11. $\dfrac{x}{15} = \dfrac{1}{5}$

12. $12 + x = 74$

13. $3x = -45$

14. $42x = -14$

15. $8x = -6$

Two-Step Equations

Two-step equations require two mathematical operations, done on both sides of the equal sign, to isolate the variable.

First, we isolate the <u>term containing the variable</u>, and then isolate the variable.

Example: Solve the equations by finding the value of the variable x.

a. $2x + 5 = 25$

   Step 1: Isolate the **term containing the variable** by subtracting 5 from both sides.

   $2x + 5 = 25$

   $2x + 5 - 5 = 25 - 5$ *Subtract 5 from both sides. (5-5=0)*

   $2x = 20$

   Step 2: Isolate the variable by dividing both sides by 2.

   $2x = 20$

   $\dfrac{2x}{2} = \dfrac{20}{2}$ *Divide both sides by 2. (2/2=1)*

   $x = 10$

b. $\dfrac{x}{3} - 4 = 8$

   Step 1: Isolate the **term containing the variable** by adding 4 to both sides.

   $\dfrac{x}{3} - 4 = 8$

   $\dfrac{x}{3} - 4 + 4 = 8 + 4$ *Add 4 to both sides. (-4+4=0)*

   $\dfrac{x}{3} = 12$

   Step 2: Isolate the variable by multiplying both sides by 3.

   $\dfrac{x}{3} = 12$

   $\dfrac{(3)x}{3} = 12(3)$ *Multiply both sides by 3. (3/3=1)*

   $x = 36$

Name _____ Date _____

Two-Step Equations

Solve for x.

1. $2x + 1 = 3$

2. $5x - 4 = 6$

3. $3x - 7 = 8$

4. $\dfrac{x}{5} + 8 = -17$

5. $1 + 7x = 15$

6. $4 + \dfrac{x}{4} = 12$

7. $8x - 1 = 3$

8. $\dfrac{x}{2} + 3 = -5$

9. $6 + 3x = 8$

10. $5 + 3x = 7$

11. $5 + 2x = -45$

12. $\dfrac{x}{5} - 7 = 23$

13. $\dfrac{x}{3} + 4 = 19$

14. $4x - 11 = 21$

15. $8 + 10x = 12$

Name _____ Date _____

Two-Step Equations

Solve for x.

1. $4x - 3 = 17$

2. $\dfrac{x}{5} + 4 = 7$

3. $10 + 2x = 52$

4. $1 + \dfrac{x}{2} = 0$

5. $8x + 11 = 13$

6. $9 + 4x = 13$

7. $5x + 15 = -30$

8. $\dfrac{x}{11} - 8 = 2$

9. $5x - 4 = 41$

10. $2 + 6x = 26$

11. $20 + 3x = -10$

12. $5 + \dfrac{x}{4} = -10$

13. $\dfrac{x}{6} - 9 = 11$

14. $\dfrac{x}{3} - 8 = 8$

15. $7x - 3 = 53$

ClayMaze.com

Equations with the Variable in a Denominator

Some equations can have the variable in a denominator and it will need to be "moved" out of the denominator in order to solve the equation.

Example: Solve the equations by finding the value of the variable x.

a. $\dfrac{2}{x} = 3$

The first step is to move the x out of the denominator by multiplying both sides by x. *It will end up on the other side of the equal sign.*

$$\dfrac{2}{x} = 3$$

$$\dfrac{(x)2}{x} = 3(x) \qquad \textit{Multiply both sides by x. (The x's cancel out: x/x = 1)}$$

$$2 = 3x$$

$$\dfrac{2}{3} = \dfrac{3x}{3} \qquad \textit{Divide both sides by 3. (The 3's cancel out: 3/3 = 1)}$$

$$\dfrac{2}{3} = x \quad \text{or} \quad x = \dfrac{2}{3}$$

b. $\dfrac{2}{5x} = 4$

The first step is to move the x out of the denominator by multiplying both sides by x.

$$\dfrac{2}{5x} = 4$$

$$\dfrac{(x)2}{5x} = 4(x) \qquad \textit{Multiply both sides by x. (The x's cancel out: x/x = 1)}$$

$$\dfrac{2}{5} = 4x$$

$$\dfrac{2}{4(5)} = \dfrac{4x}{4} \qquad \textit{Divide both sides by 4. (The 4's cancel out: 4/4 = 1)}$$

$$\dfrac{1}{10} = x \quad \text{or} \quad x = \dfrac{1}{10}$$

Example: Solve the equation by finding the value of the variable x.

$$\frac{2}{3x} - 8 = 2$$

The first step is to isolate the **term containing the variable**, and the next step is to isolate the variable itself.

Step 1: Isolate the term containing the variable by adding 8 to both sides

$$\frac{2}{3x} - 8 = 2$$

$$\frac{2}{3x} - 8 + 8 = 2 + 8 \qquad \text{Add 8 to both sides to isolate the term containing the variable.}$$

$$\frac{2}{3x} = 10$$

Step 2: Move the x out of the denominator by multiplying both sides by x. Then isolate the x.

$$\frac{(x)2}{3x} = 10(x) \qquad \text{Multiply both sides by x. (The x's cancel out: x/x = 1)}$$

$$\frac{2}{3} = 10x$$

$$\frac{2}{10(3)} = \frac{10x}{10} \qquad \text{Divide both sides by 10. (The 10's cancel out: 10/10 = 1)}$$

$$\frac{2}{30} = x$$

$$\frac{1}{15} = x \quad \text{or} \quad x = \frac{1}{15}$$

Name _____ Date _____

Equations with the Variable in a Denominator

Solve for x.

1. $\dfrac{4}{x} = 2$

2. $\dfrac{5}{x} = 8$

3. $\dfrac{12}{x} = 6$

4. $3 = \dfrac{6}{x}$

5. $\dfrac{14}{x} = -7$

6. $5 = \dfrac{2}{x}$

7. $\dfrac{1}{5x} = 1$

8. $\dfrac{9}{5x} = -2$

9. $\dfrac{5}{2x} + 4 = -1$

10. $5 + \dfrac{6}{x} = 7$

11. $8 = \dfrac{4}{3x}$

12. $\dfrac{3}{4x} = -2$

13. $\dfrac{1}{2x} - 4 = 1$

14. $\dfrac{2}{3x} + 4 = 9$

15. $\dfrac{2}{3x} + 7 = 1$

116   ClayMaze.com

Name _____ Date _____

Equations with the Variable in a Denominator

Solve for x.

1. $\dfrac{7}{x} = 1$

2. $\dfrac{3}{x} = -4$

3. $\dfrac{2}{x} = 12$

4. $8 = \dfrac{4}{x}$

5. $\dfrac{11}{x} = -11$

6. $1 + \dfrac{10}{x} = 3$

7. $\dfrac{3}{4x} = 1$

8. $\dfrac{2}{11x} = 10$

9. $5 = \dfrac{6}{7x} - 1$

10. $\dfrac{8}{x} - 3 = -7$

11. $\dfrac{12}{5x} = 4$

12. $\dfrac{4}{3x} = 3$

13. $\dfrac{3}{4x} + 5 = 2$

14. $\dfrac{4}{7x} - 6 = -10$

15. $\dfrac{1}{5x} + 4 = 8$

ClayMaze.com

Combining Like Terms to Solve Equations

When there are multiple terms containing the variable in an equation, like terms should be combined first in order to solve the equation.

Example: Solve for x.

a. $4x - 7 = 3 + 5x$ There are two terms in this equation containing the variable: $4x$ and $5x$. These can be combined, but they need to be on the same side of the equal sign to do this.

$$4x - 7 = 3 + 5x$$

$$4x - 7 - 5x = 3 + 5x - 5x$$ *Subtract 5x from both sides to get both variable terms on the same side of the equal sign.*

$$-x - 7 = 3$$ *Combine like terms. ($4x - 5x = -x$)*

$$-x - 7 + 7 = 3 + 7$$ *Isolate the variable by adding 7 to both sides.*

$$-x = 10$$

$$-x(-1) = 10(-1)$$ *Multiply each side by -1 to get rid of the negative sign in front of x.*

$$x = -10$$

b. $8x - 5 + x = 4 + 3x - x - 2$

$\underbrace{8x - 5 + x}_{9x - 5} = \underbrace{4 + 3x - x - 2}_{2 + 2x}$ *Combine like terms on each side of the equation.*

$$9x - 5 = 2 + 2x$$

$$9x - 5 - 2x = 2 + 2x - 2x$$ *Subtract 2x from both sides to get the variable terms on the same side of the equal sign and combine like terms.*

$$7x - 5 = 2$$ *Combine like terms. ($9x - 2x = 7x$)*

$$7x - 5 + 5 = 2 + 5$$ *Isolate the term containing the variable by adding 5 to both sides.*

$$7x = 7$$

$$\frac{7x}{7} = \frac{7}{7}$$ *Divide each side by 7 to isolate x.*

$$x = 1$$

Name _____ Date _____

Combining Like Terms to Solve Equations

Solve for x.

1. $2x + 3 = 5 + x$

2. $3x - 1 = 6 - 4x$

3. $5 + 2x = 3x - 1$

4. $2x - 7 + 8x = 2x + 9$

5. $4x + 2 + x = 1 - 2x$

6. $4 + 5x = 3x - 7 + x$

7. $1 + 5x + 3 = 4x - 8 - 2x$

8. $3x + 2 - 2x = 2 + 6x - 5$

9. $3 + 2x - 1 + 4x = 8 - 5x - 10 + 7$

10. $4x - 6 + x + 2 = 10 - 7x + 6 + 2x$

119

ClayMaze.com

Name _____ Date _____

Combining Like Terms to Solve Equations

Solve for x.

1. $7x - 8 = 3x + 4$

2. $2x - 7 = 9 + 10x$

3. $4 - 3x = 12 - 5x$

4. $4x - 2 + 3x = 8 - 3x$

5. $5 + 2x - 3 = 7 - 6x$

6. $5x + 8 - 2x = 10 + 2x$

7. $1 + 3x - 4 = 4x + 7 - 2x$

8. $3x + 2 - x = 5 + 4x + 11$

9. $4x + 7 + 5x - 1 = 5 + 2x - 3 + 3x$

10. $5 - 3x + 9 + 4x = 7 - 2x + 3 + 8x$

Points, Lines and the Coordinate Plane

The Coordinate Plane, Points, Lines, Distance Formula, Midpoint Formula, Slope, Intercepts, Linear Equations

The Coordinate Plane

To set up a rectangular coordinate plane, draw two perpendicular number lines, one horizontal and one vertical, intersecting at the 0 point of each one.

The horizontal line is the **x-axis** and the vertical line is the **y-axis**. Their point of intersection is the **origin**. These x and y axes divide the coordinate plane into **4 quadrants**: I, II, III and IV.

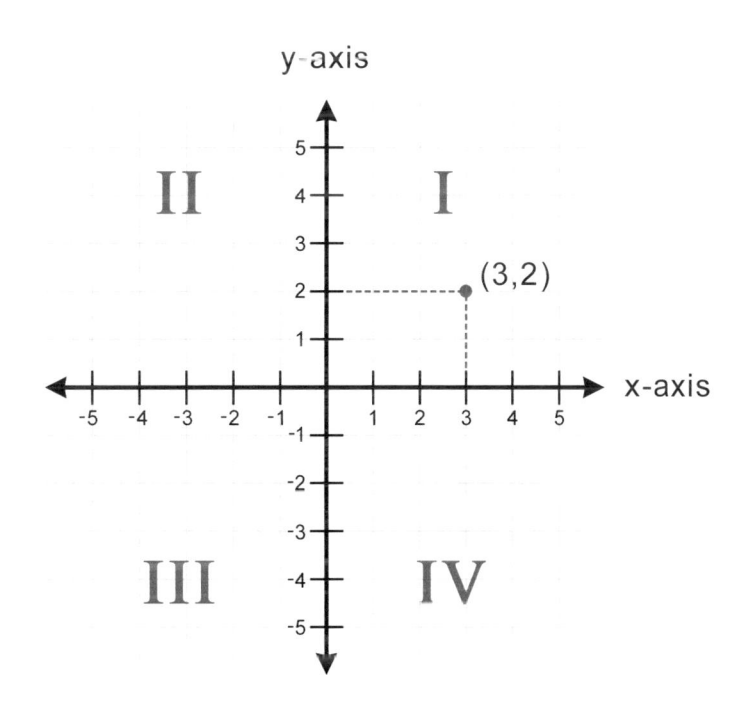

Notice the numbers on the right half of the x-axis and the top half of the y-axis are positive, while those on the left half of the x-axis and the bottom half of the y-axis are negative.

Plotting Points

Points are plotted on the coordinate plane using ordered pairs. An ordered pair consists of two numbers. The first is the x-coordinate and the second is the y-coordinate.

If you were to draw a vertical line through the x-coordinate on the x-axis and a horizontal line through the y-coordinate on the y-axis, the point is plotted at their point of intersection.
See the point (3,2) in the figure above.

Example: Plot the points and indicate which quadrant each belongs to.

A. (2,4)   Quadrant: __I__
C. (-5,-5) Quadrant: __III__
E. (-3,5) Quadrant: __II__
B. (-1,2) Quadrant: __II__
D. (3,-4) Quadrant: __IV__
F. (4,-3) Quadrant: __IV__

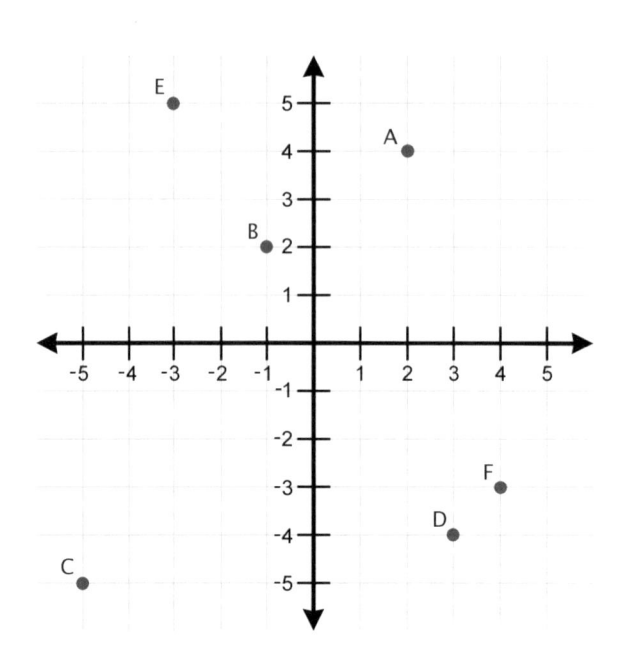

Example: Find the coordinates for the points shown below.

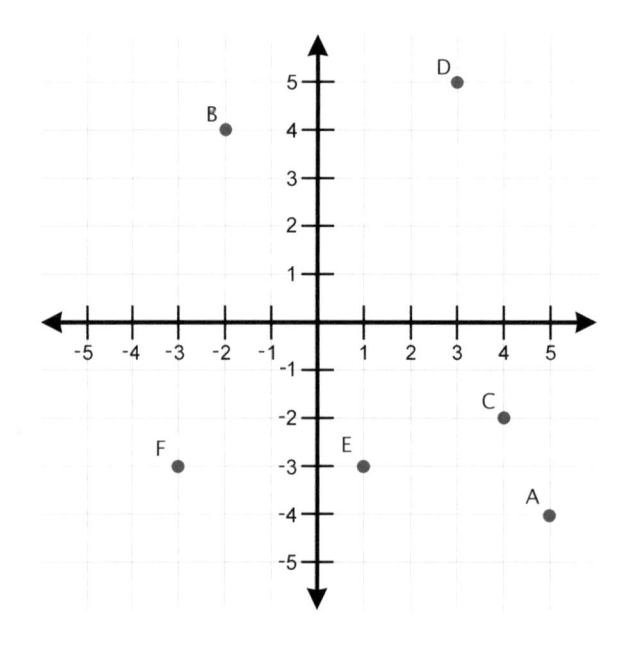

A. __(5,-4)__   B. __(-2,4)__   C. __(4,-2)__   D. __(3,5)__   E. __(1,-3)__   F. __(-3,-3)__

Name _____   Date _____

The Coordinate Plane

Plot and label the points. Indicate which quadrant each one belongs to.

A (2, 3)   Quadrant: _____
B (−2, 5)   Quadrant: _____
C (−3, −4)   Quadrant: _____
D (1, −5)   Quadrant: _____
E (4, 1)   Quadrant: _____
F (−3, 1)   Quadrant: _____
G (−1, 6)   Quadrant: _____
H (5, 4)   Quadrant: _____
I (5, −2)   Quadrant: _____
J (−2, −2)   Quadrant: _____
K (2, −3)   Quadrant: _____
L (−4, 3)   Quadrant: _____

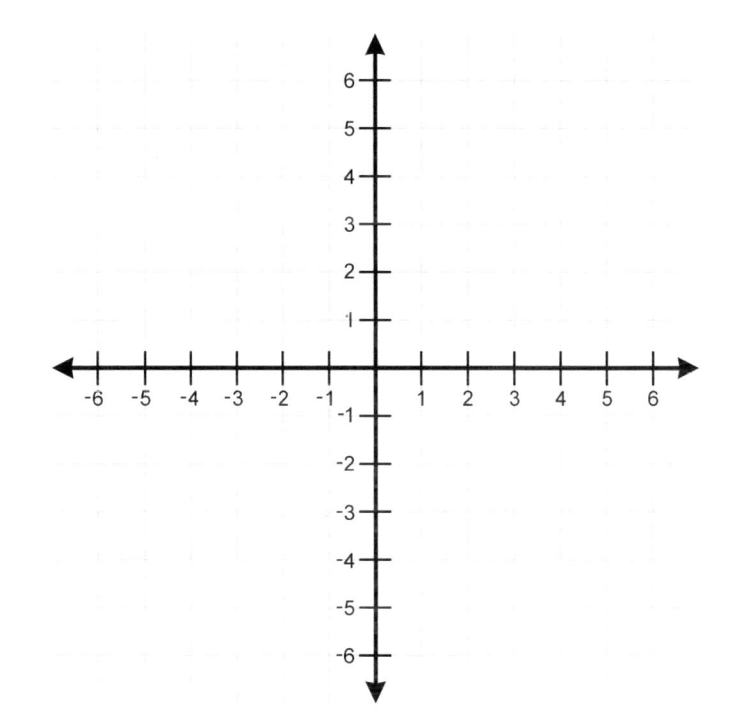

Write the coordinates for the plotted points.

A _____   I _____
B _____   J _____
C _____   K _____
D _____   L _____
E _____   M _____
F _____   N _____
G _____   O _____
H _____   P _____

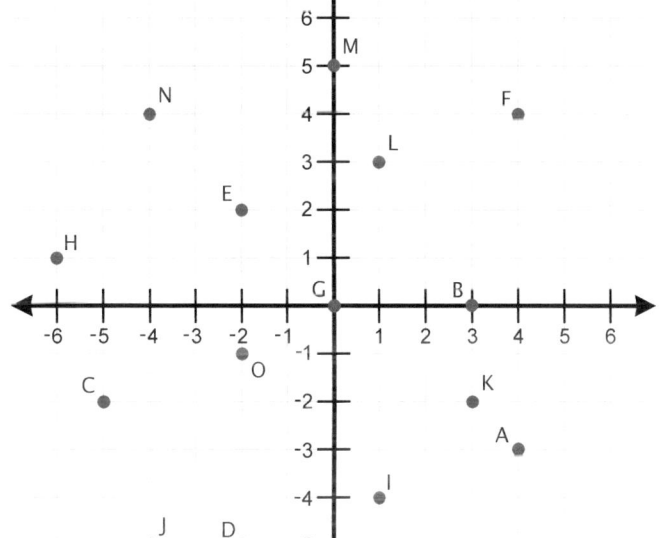

123   ClayMaze.com

Name _____   Date _____

The Coordinate Plane

Plot and label the points. Indicate which quadrant each one belongs to.

A	(1, 1)	Quadrant: _____
B	(3, −5)	Quadrant: _____
C	(−5, 3)	Quadrant: _____
D	(2, 6)	Quadrant: _____
E	(−4, −4)	Quadrant: _____
F	(3, −2)	Quadrant: _____
G	(1, −6)	Quadrant: _____
H	(−2, 5)	Quadrant: _____
I	(4, 3)	Quadrant: _____
J	(−4, 1)	Quadrant: _____
K	(−2, −6)	Quadrant: _____
L	(−3, −2)	Quadrant: _____

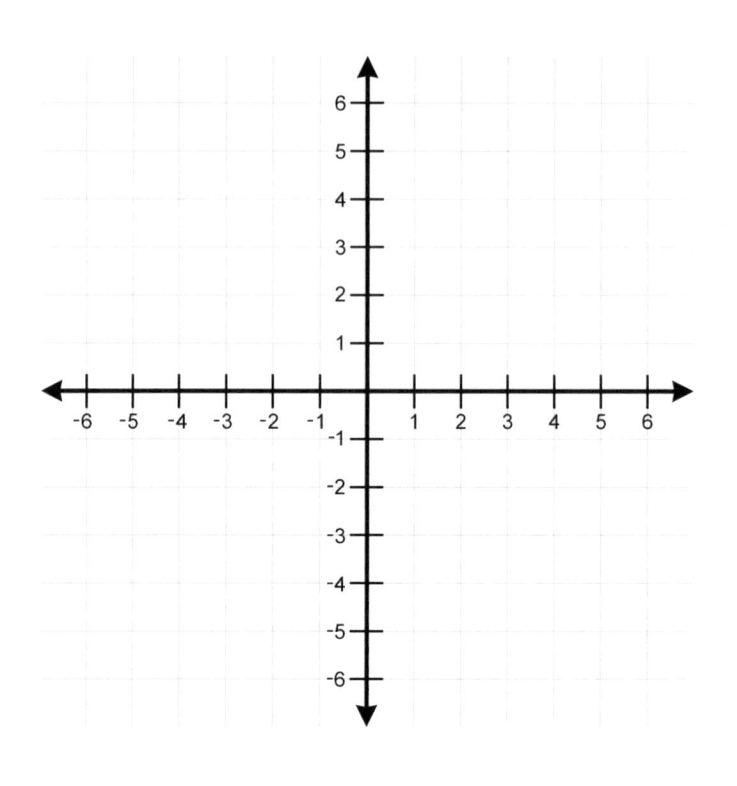

Write the coordinates for the plotted points.

A _____   I _____
B _____   J _____
C _____   K _____
D _____   L _____
E _____   M _____
F _____   N _____
G _____   O _____
H _____   P _____

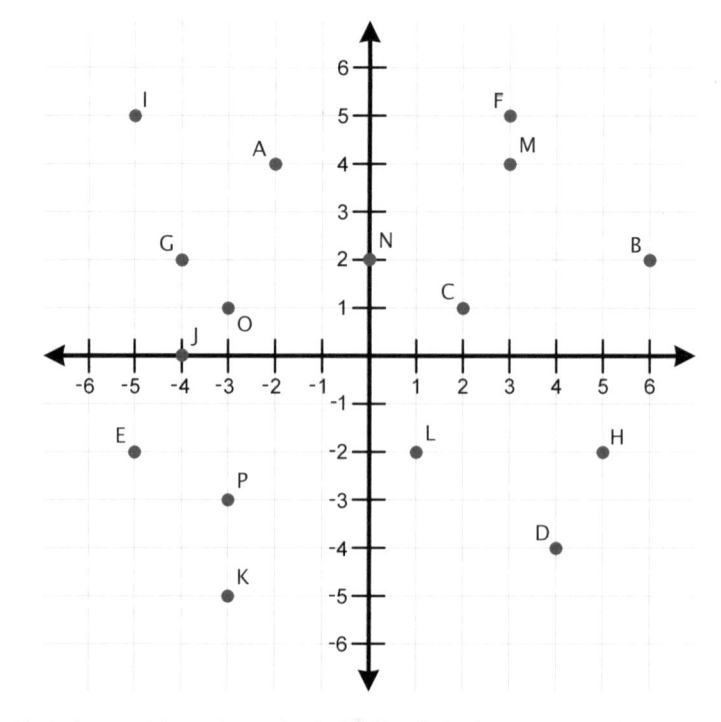

124   ClayMaze.com

Distances

When two points share the same x-coordinate or y-coordinate, the distance can often be determined by just counting the units between them.

Example: Find the distance between the points in each pair.

Point A: (1,2)
Point B: (5,2)
Distance between A and B: 4 units

Point C: (1,−2)
Point D: (−4,−2)
Distance between C and D: 5 units

Point E: (−3,1)
Point F: (−3,5)
Distance between E and F: 4 units

Point G: (−5,4)
Point H: (−5,−4)
Distance between G and H: 8 units

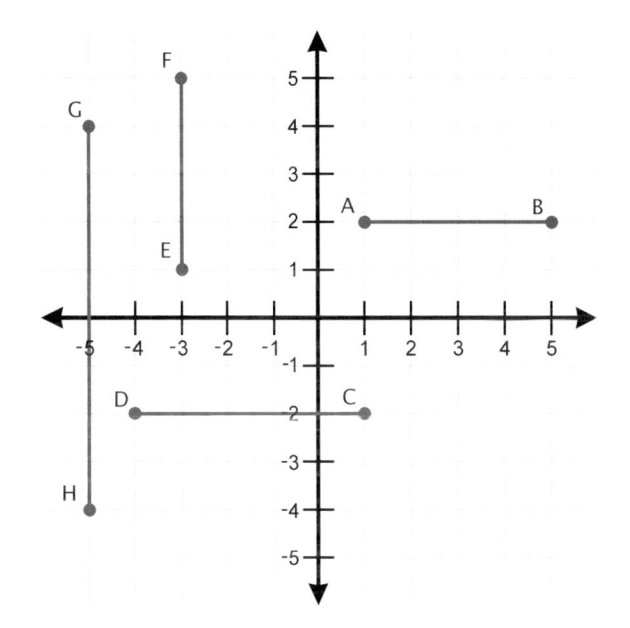

Example: Find the points.

a. Plot and label the Point A: (2,4)

   Point B is 3 units to the right of Point A.

   Coordinates of Point B. (1,4)

b. Plot and label the Point C: (−4,5)

   Point D is 7 units below Point C.

   Coordinates of Point D: (−4,−2)

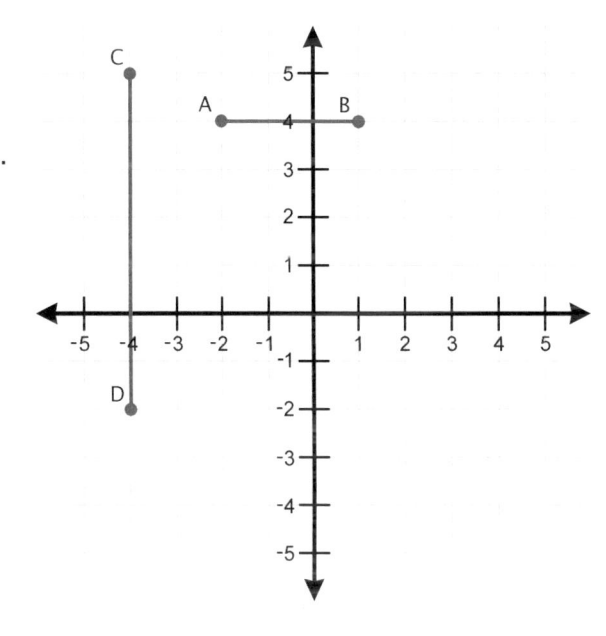

Name _____   Date _____

Distance

Plot the points with lines connecting each pair and find the distance between each pair of points.

A: (2,4) **B:** (6,4)
Distance: _____

C: (−3,−2) **D:** (3,−2)
Distance: _____

E: (1,2) **F:** (1,−6)
Distance: _____

G: (−5,5) **H:** (−1,5)
Distance: _____

I: (−6,−5) **J:** (−6,4)
Distance: _____

K: (−2,1) **L:** (3,1)
Distance: _____

M: (−5,1) **N:** (−5,−6)
Distance: _____

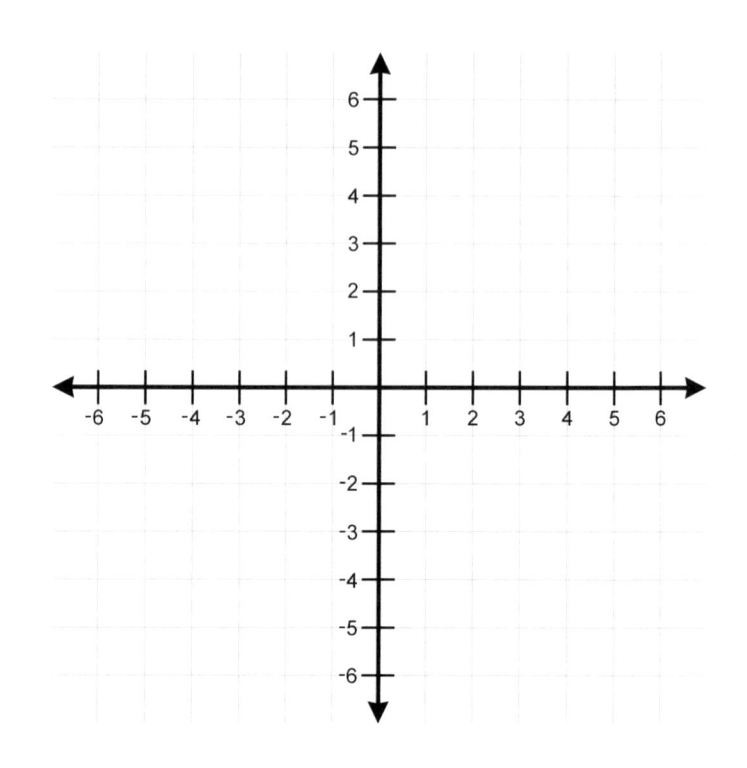

Find the missing points and plot the pairs, drawing lines connecting each pair.

A: (1,3) **B:** _____
Point B is 5 units below **A**.

C: (−1,−4) **D:** _____
Point D is 3 units to the left of **C**.

E: (−6,5) **F:** _____
Point F is 8 units to the right of **E**.

G: (−2,−3) **H:** _____
Point H is 6 units above **G**.

I: (3,−6) **J:** _____
Point J is 5 units to the left of **I**.

K: (5,2) **L:** _____
Point L is 4 units above **K**.

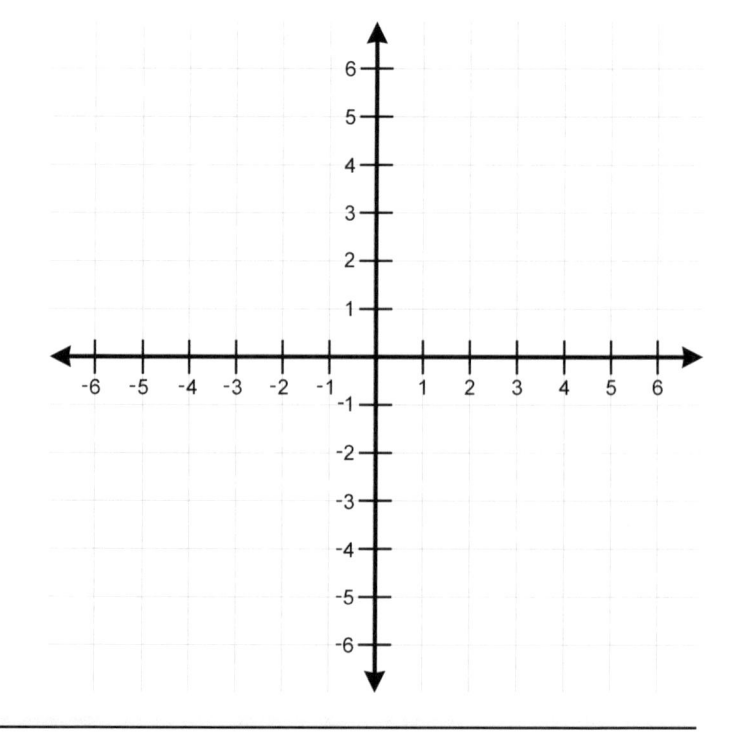

The Distance Formula

The distance between two points on a coordinate plane can be found using the **distance formula**. This is useful when the two points don't share the same x-coordinate or y-coordinate.

The Distance Formula

If P and Q are two points on a coordinate plane, with P at position (x_1, y_1) and Q at position (x_2, y_2), the **distance** between points P and Q is:

$$d = \sqrt{(x_2 - x_1)^2 + (y_2 - y_1)^2}$$

Example: Find the distance between the given points using the distance formula.

Point A: (−4, −3)
Point B: (2, 5)

Using the distance formula:

$$d = \sqrt{(x_2 - x_1)^2 + (y_2 - y_1)^2}$$

with Point A: (−4, −3) as (x_1, y_1)
and Point B: (2, 5) as (x_2, y_2),

$$d = \sqrt{(2 - {-4})^2 + (5 - {-3})^2}$$

$$= \sqrt{(2 + 4)^2 + (5 + 3)^2}$$

$$= \sqrt{(6)^2 + (8)^2}$$

$$= \sqrt{36 + 64}$$

$$= \sqrt{100}$$

$$= 10$$

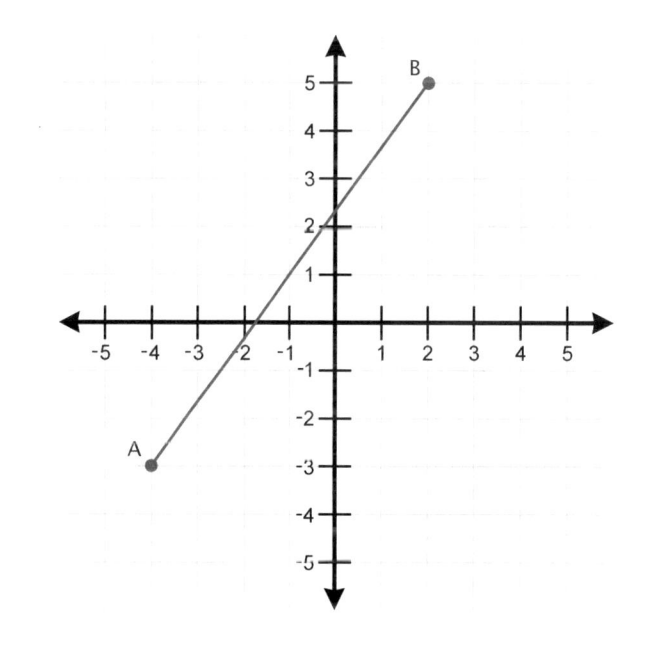

Distance between A and B: 10 units

Example: Find the distance between the given points using the distance formula.

Point A: (−2, −3)
Point B: (−5, 1)

Using the distance formula:

$$d = \sqrt{(x_2 - x_1)^2 + (y_2 - y_1)^2}$$

with Point A: (−2, −3) as (x_1, y_1)
and Point B: (−5, 1) as (x_2, y_2),

$$d = \sqrt{(-5 - -2)^2 + (1 - -3)^2}$$

$$= \sqrt{(-5 + 2)^2 + (1 + 3)^2}$$

$$= \sqrt{(-3)^2 + (4)^2}$$

$$= \sqrt{9 + 16}$$

$$= \sqrt{25}$$

$$= 5$$

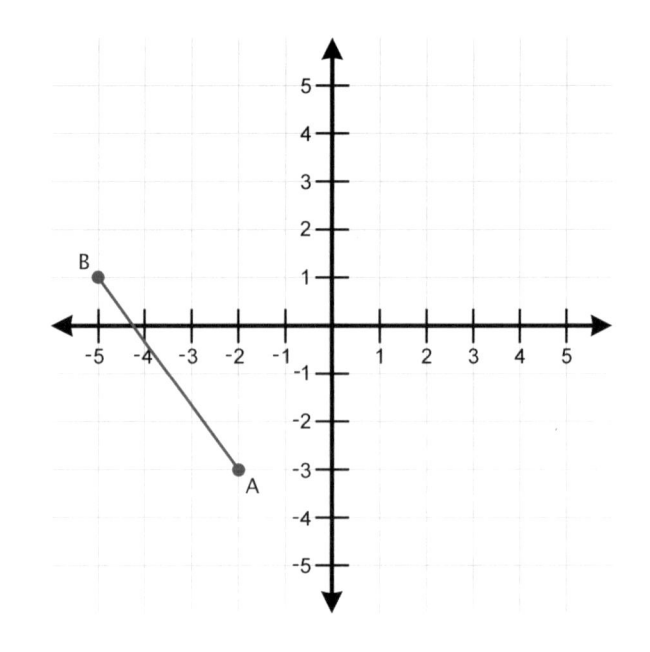

Distance between A and B: 5 units

Name _____ Date _____

The Distance Formula

Find the distance between each pair of points using the distance formula.

1. (−5,−2) and (3,4)

2. (2,1) and (5,5)

3. (2,5) and (2,−2)

4. (4,11) and (−8,−5)

5. (−3,8) and (7,8)

6. (2, 2) and (11,14)

7. (−4,4) and (−7,8)

8. (−4,−3) and (5,9)

9. (−2,−3) and (−5,1)

ClayMaze.com

Name _____   Date _____

The Distance Formula

Find the distance between each pair of points using the distance formula.

1. (−1,7) and (−1,3)	2. (5,−4) and (−3,2)	3. (2,0) and (−1,−4)
4. (1,−2) and (−4,10)	5. (10,−4) and (−6,8)	6. (1,1) and (−7,7)
7. (−8,−7) and (4,9)	8. (5,5) and (1,8)	9. (−11,4) and (1,−5)

Midpoint Formula

The midpoint formula is used to find the midpoint of the line segment connecting two points on the coordinate plane. This point is halfway between the two end points.

The Midpoint Formula

The **midpoint** between the two points A and B on a coordinate plane, where A is located at position (x_1, y_1) and B is located at position (x_2, y_2), is:

$$\text{midpoint} = \left(\frac{x_1 + x_2}{2}, \frac{y_1 + y_2}{2}\right)$$

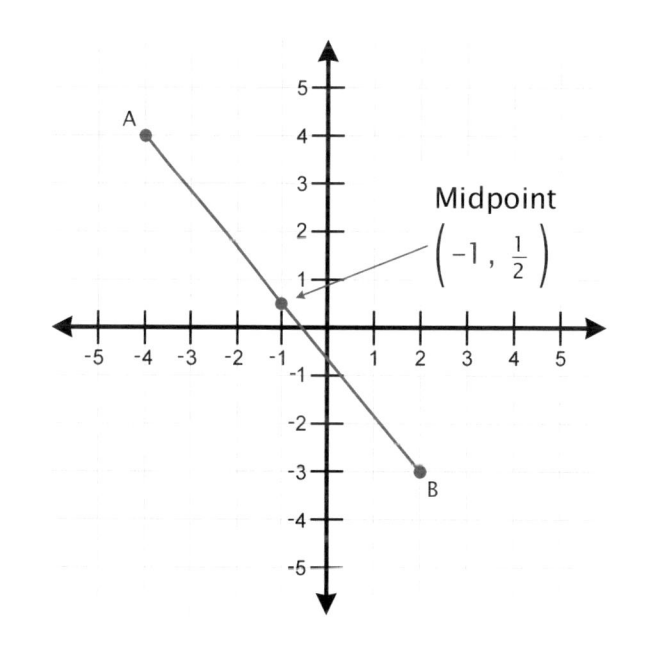

Example: Find the midpoint between the given points.

Point A: (−4, 4)
Point B: (2, −3)

Using the midpoint formula:

$$\text{midpoint} = \left(\frac{x_1 + x_2}{2}, \frac{y_1 + y_2}{2}\right)$$

with Point A: (−4, 4) as (x_1, y_1)
and Point B: (2, −3) as (x_2, y_2),

substitute the values into the formula:

$$\text{midpoint} = \left(\frac{-4 + 2}{2}, \frac{4 + {-3}}{2}\right)$$

$$\text{midpoint} = \left(\frac{-2}{2}, \frac{1}{2}\right)$$

$$\text{midpoint} = \left(-1, \frac{1}{2}\right)$$

Midpoint $\left(-1, \frac{1}{2}\right)$

Example: Find the midpoint between the given points.

Point A: (−1, −2)
Point B: (3, 5)

Using the midpoint formula:

$$\text{midpoint} = \left(\frac{x_1 + x_2}{2}, \frac{y_1 + y_2}{2} \right)$$

with Point A: (−1, −2) as (x_1, y_1)
and Point B: (3, 5) as (x_2, y_2),

substitute the values into the formula:

$$\text{midpoint} = \left(\frac{-1 + 3}{2}, \frac{-2 + 5}{2} \right)$$

$$\text{midpoint} = \left(\frac{2}{2}, \frac{3}{2} \right)$$

$$\text{midpoint} = \left(1, 1\frac{1}{2} \right)$$

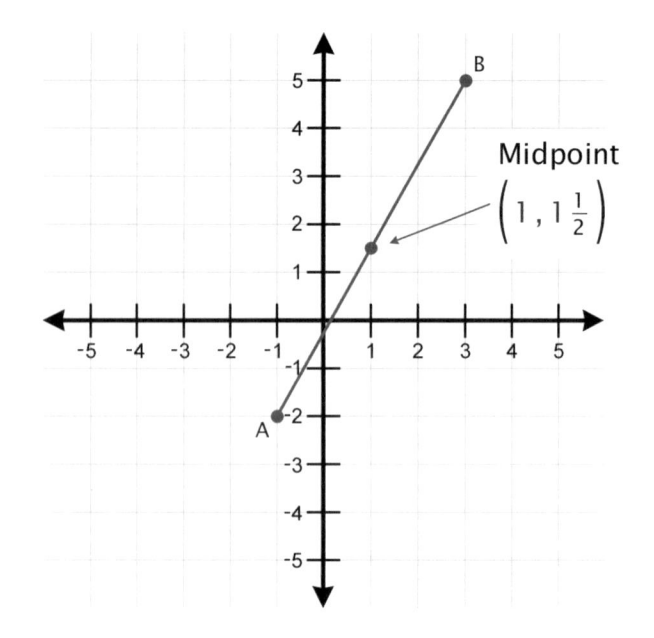

Midpoint $\left(1, 1\frac{1}{2} \right)$

Name _____ Date _____

Midpoint

Find the endpoints and midpoints for the line segments and plot the midpoints.

A: _____ B: _____

Midpoint: _____

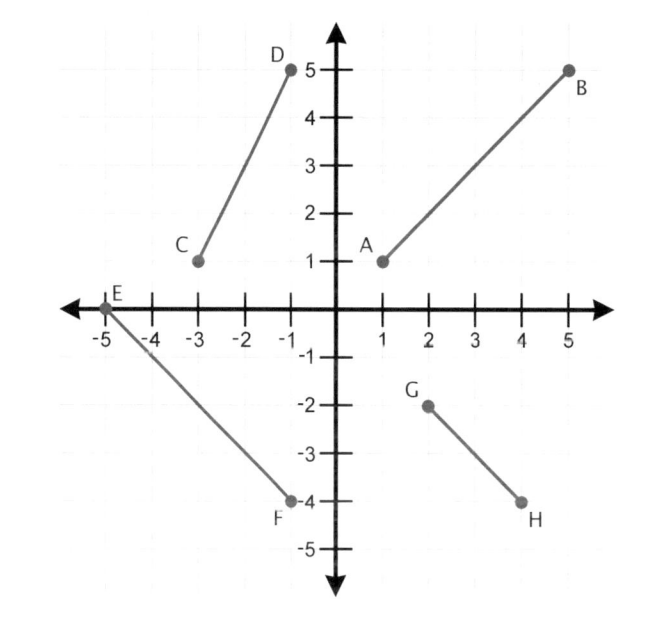

C: _____ D: _____

Midpoint: _____

E: _____ F: _____

Midpoint: _____

G: _____ H: _____

Midpoint: _____

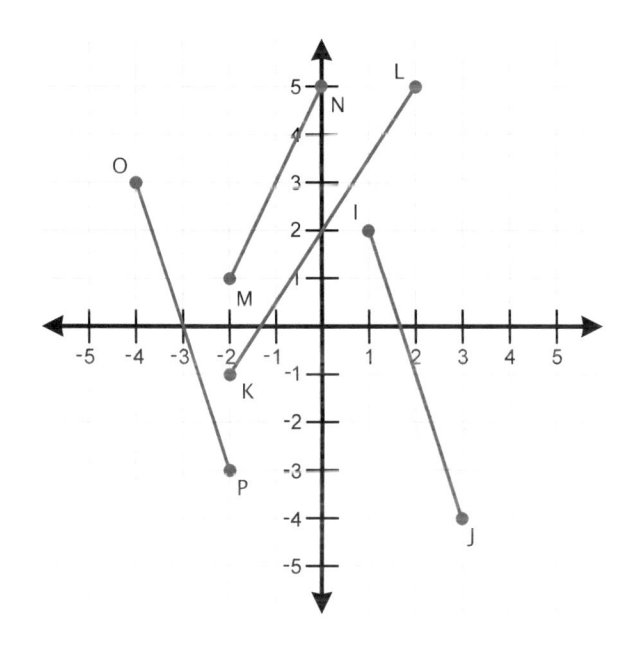

I: _____ J: _____

Midpoint: _____

K: _____ L: _____

Midpoint: _____

M: _____ N: _____

Midpoint: _____

O: _____ P: _____

Midpoint: _____

133 ClayMaze.com

Name _____ Date _____

Midpoint

Find the midpoint for each pair of points using the midpoint formula.

1. (0,−1) and (4,3)	2. (−4,−1) and (2,3)	3. (−5,−1) and (−2,5)
4. (2,−2) and (−3,−4)	5. (1,2) and (4,4)	6. (−3,−5) and (2,1)
7. (−2,−1) and (2,−5)	8. (−4,−1) and (−1,7)	9. (0,4) and (4,0)
10. (−2,−5) and (3,−1)	11. (2,−1) and (−2,−3)	12. (−8,−8) and (8,8)

Slope

The slope of a line describes the steepness of a line. It can be positive (upward from left to right), negative (downward from left to right) or zero (horizontal). The slope of a vertical line is considered "undefined".

Finding the Slope of a Line

When looking at a graph, if two points are known on a line, one way to find its slope is to count the **vertical difference (rise)** and **horizontal difference (run)** between the two points and place them into a rise over run format. Then determine the sign based on how the line is angled.

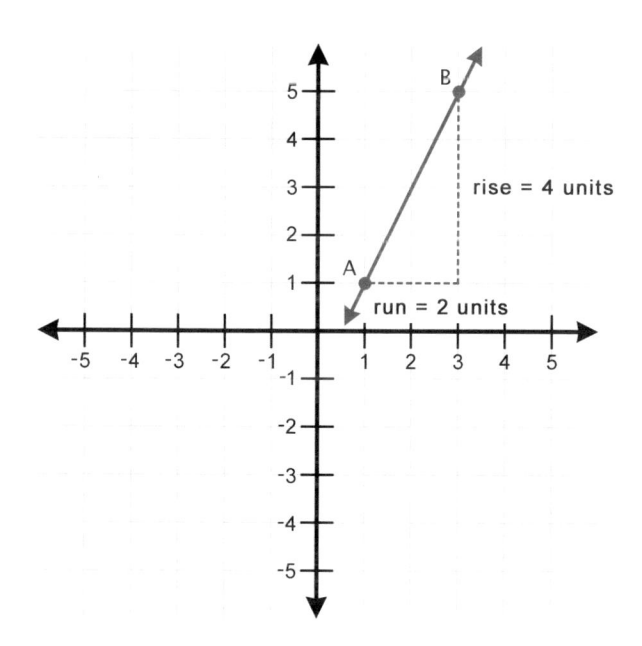

$$\text{slope} = \frac{\text{rise}}{\text{run}}$$

The slope of the line shown is 2:

$$\text{slope} = \frac{4}{2} = 2$$

Since the line is angled upward, the slope has a positive value.

Steps to finding the slope of a line on a coordinate plane (given two points):

1. **Find the rise** - count the units in the y direction between the two points.

2. **Find the run** - count the units in the x direction between the two points.

3. **Find the magnitude of the slope** - Write it as rise over run: $\frac{\text{rise}}{\text{run}}$

4. **Determine the sign:**

   If the line is pointing downward from left to right, the slope is **negative**.
   If the line is pointing upward from left to right, the slope is **positive**.

Example: Find the slope of the line passing through the points A and B.

Point A: (−4, 3)   **Point B:** (−2, −2)

The vertical distance between Point A and Point B is 5 units: **rise = 5**.

The horizontal distance between Point A and Point B is 2 units: **run = 2**.

$$\frac{\text{rise}}{\text{run}} = \frac{5}{2}$$

The line is angled downward from left to right, so the slope has a **negative** value.

$$\text{slope} = -\frac{5}{2}$$

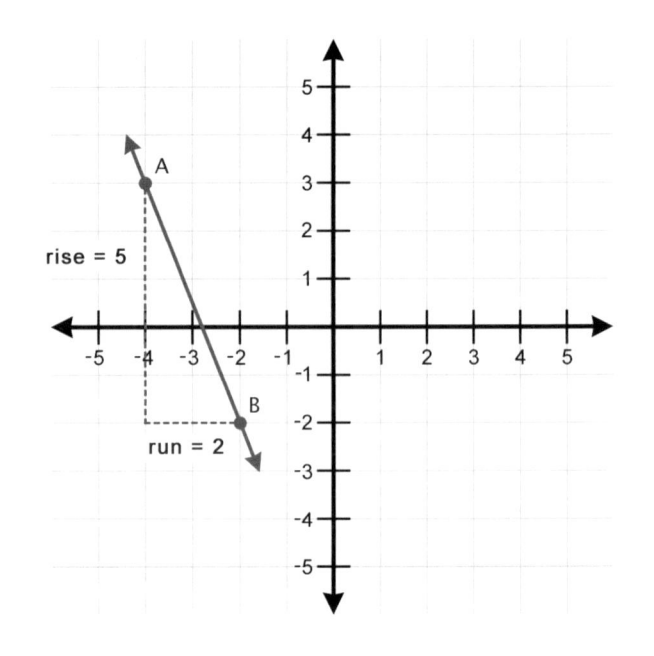

If the slope is an improper fraction (denominator > numerator), it's better to leave it in that format than to convert it to a mixed number, since it shows the rise and run values.

Example: Find the slope of the line passing through the points C and D.

Point C: (−3, 2)   **Point D:** (4, 2)

The slope of a horizontal line is zero.

There is no vertical difference between the two points on the line: **rise = 0**.

The horizontal distance between Point C and Point D is 7: **run = 7**.

$$\frac{\text{rise}}{\text{run}} = \frac{0}{7} = 0 \qquad \text{slope} = 0$$

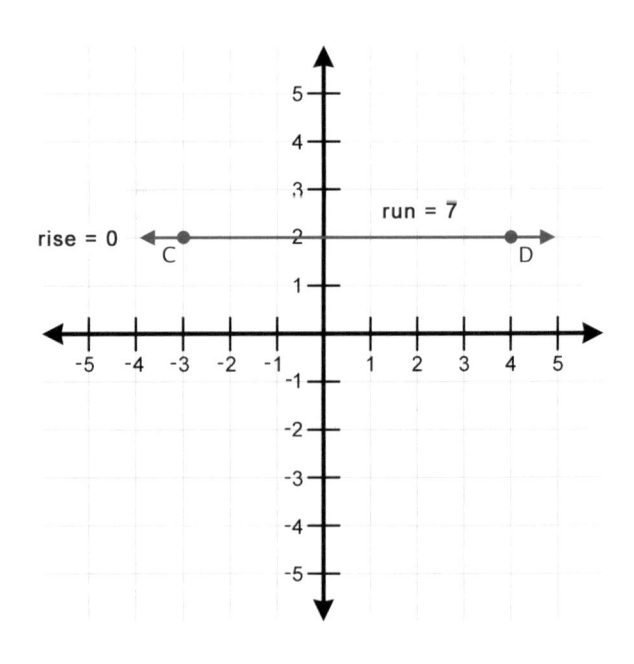

Name _____   Date _____

Slope

Find the coordinates of the points and the slope of the lines passing through each pair.

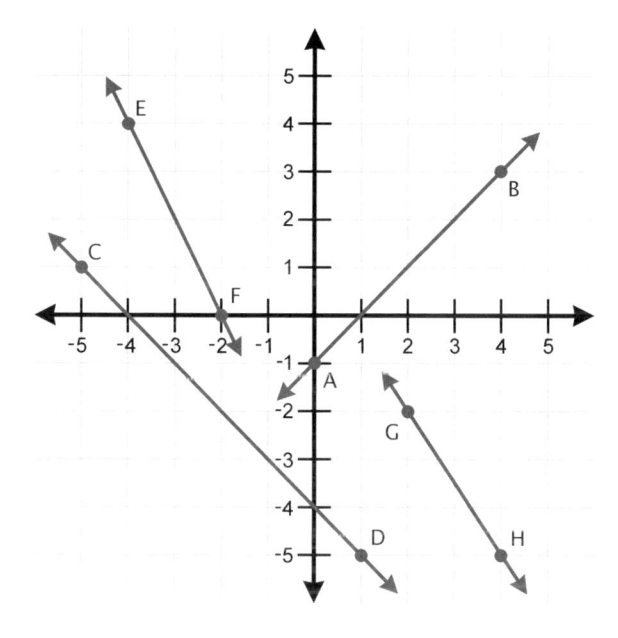

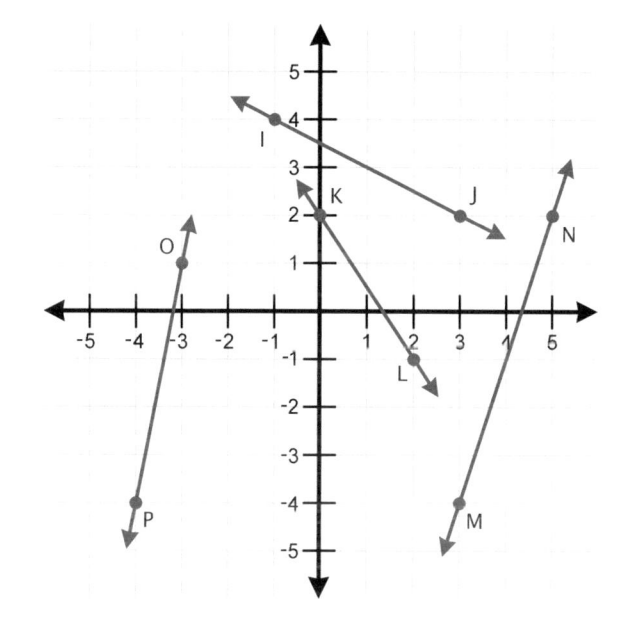

A: _____   B: _____

Slope:

C: _____   D: _____

Slope:

E: _____   F: _____

Slope:

G: _____   H: _____

Slope:

I: _____   J: _____

Slope:

K: _____   L: _____

Slope:

M: _____   N: _____

Slope:

O: _____   P: _____

Slope:

137   ClayMaze.com

Name _____ Date _____

Slope

Plot the points and draw lines passing through each given pair. Find the slope of the lines.

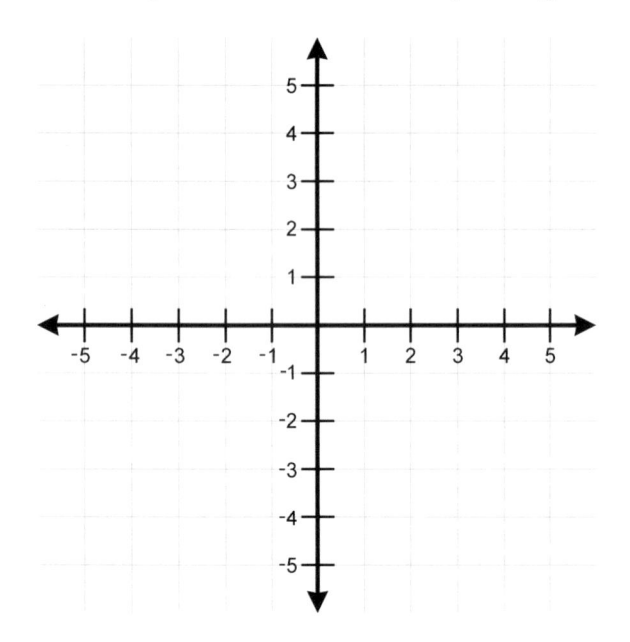

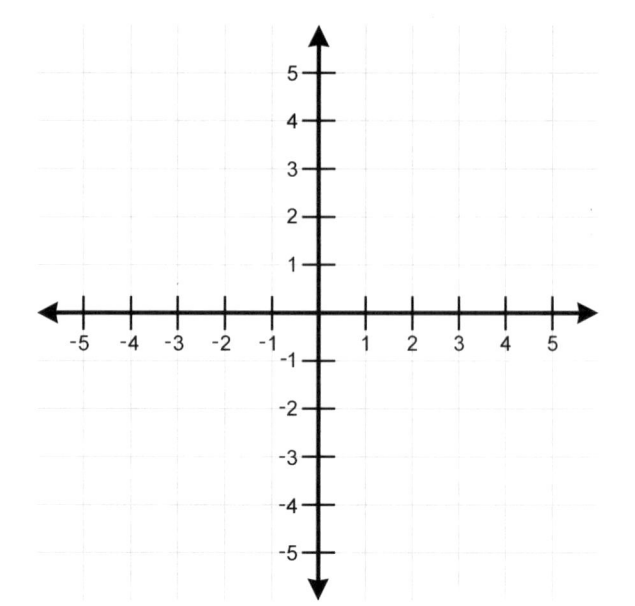

A: (−1, 5)   B: (1, 2)
Slope:

I: (−4, 3)   J: (3, 4)
Slope:

C: (0, −2)   D: (2, 0)
Slope:

K: (3, 2)   L: (4, −5)
Slope:

E: (−2, −3)   F: (4, −5)
Slope:

M: (−3, 1)   N: (1, 1)
Slope:

G: (−4, −5)   H: (−3, 3)
Slope:

O: (1, −1)   P: (−2, −5)
Slope:

ClayMaze.com

Finding the Slope of a Line Using the Slope Formula

The slope of a line can also be found using a formula without the need for counting units as long as two points are known. **The formula accounts for the sign of the slope, so it's important to pay attention to signs in the calculation.**

Slope

The slope of a non-vertical line connecting two points P and Q in a coordinate plane where P is located at position (x_1, y_1) and Q is located at position (x_2, y_2) is:

$$m = \frac{y_2 - y_1}{x_2 - x_1}$$

(m is commonly used to stand for slope.)

$y_2 - y_1$ is the vertical difference between the two points.
$x_2 - x_1$ is the horizontal difference between the two points.

Example: Find the slope of the line passing through the given points.

Point A: (-1, -3)
Point B: (4, 2)

Using the slope formula: $m = \dfrac{y_2 - y_1}{x_2 - x_1}$

with Point A: (-1, -3) as (x_1, y_1)
and Point B: (4, 2) as (x_2, y_2)

$$m = \frac{2 - {-3}}{4 - {-1}} = \frac{5}{5} = 1$$

The slope is 1, which is positive, so it is an upward slope.

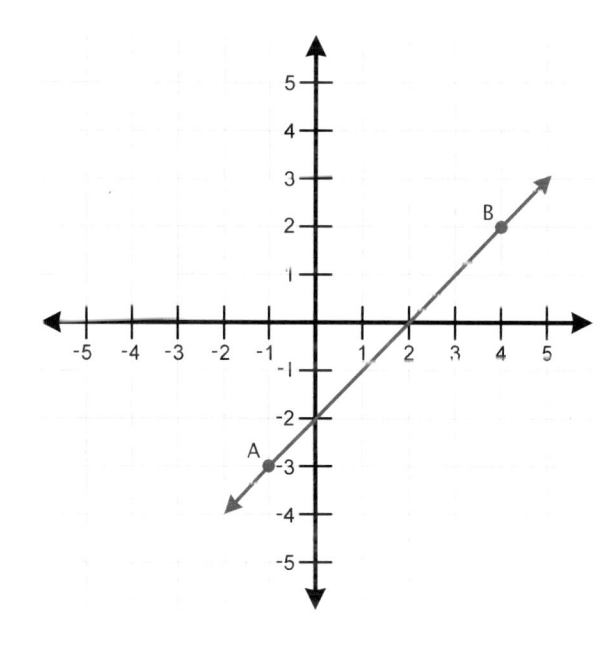

139

Example: Find the slope of the line passing through the given points.

Point C: (1, 4)
Point D: (3, -2)

Using the slope formula: $m = \dfrac{y_2 - y_1}{x_2 - x_1}$

with Point C: (1, 4) as (x_1, y_1)
and Point D: (3, -2) as (x_2, y_2)

$$m = \dfrac{-2 - 4}{3 - 1} = \dfrac{-6}{2} = -3$$

The slope is -3, which is negative, so it is a downward slope.

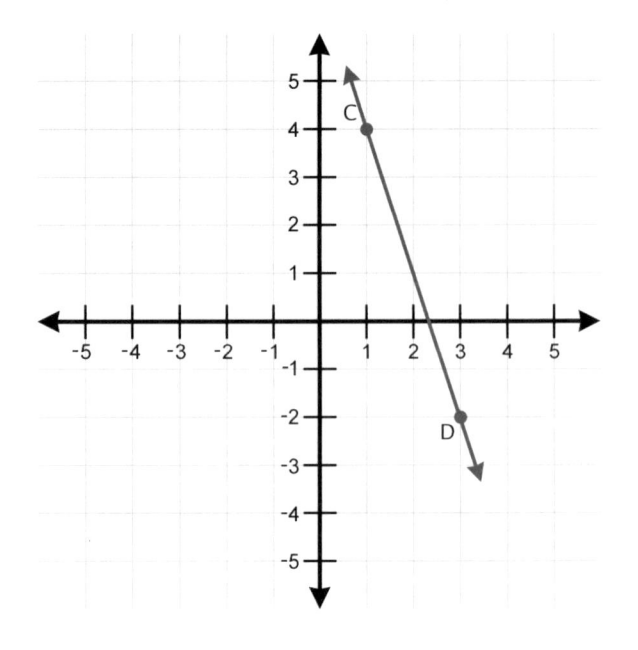

Example: Find the slope of the line passing through the given points.

Point E: (-2, 4)
Point F: (3, 4)

Using the slope formula: $m = \dfrac{y_2 - y_1}{x_2 - x_1}$

with Point C: (-2, 4) as (x_1, y_1)
and Point D: (3, 4) as (x_2, y_2)

$$m = \dfrac{4 - 4}{3 - {-2}} = \dfrac{0}{5} = 0$$

The slope is 0, so this is a horizontal line.

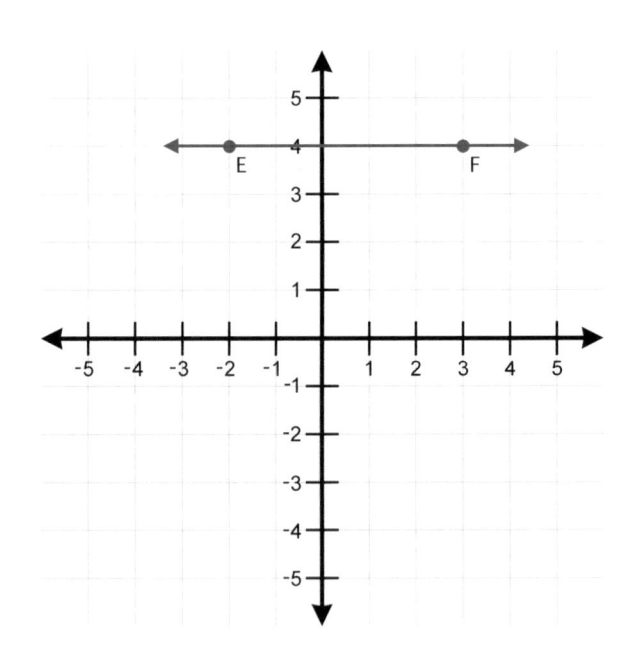

Name _____   Date _____

Slope

Find the slope of the line that passes through each pair of points.

1. (1,−4) and (5,−2)	2. (0,−4) and (2,4)	3. (−2,2) and (4,6)
4. (4,2) and (3,5)	5. (2,−3) and (0,−7)	6. (1,−6) and (7,2)
7. (−4,−5) and (1,−5)	8. (1,8) and (5,0)	9. (−1,3) and (−5,5)
10. (−8,0) and (4,6)	11. (−2,−2) and (2,2)	12. (−1,−1) and (4,1)

Name _____ Date _____

Slope

Find the slope of the line that passes through each pair of points.

1. (−5,1) and (−4,−3)	2. (−4,0) and (1,2)	3. (−2,−1) and (2,−7)
4. (1,4) and (−3,−2)	5. (−1,−3) and (4,−4)	6. (5,4) and (−6,4)
7. (−3,−3) and (4,−1)	8. (−7,4) and (−3,2)	9. (−1,0) and (1,6)
10. (3,2) and (4,5)	11. (5,3) and (−2,−4)	12. (0,1) and (−5,−4)

Linear Equations and Intercepts

A linear equation describes a straight line and the coordinate plane can be used to visualize it. Below is an example of a linear equation.

y = 2x + 4

Intercepts
The point at which the line passes through the x-axis is called the **x-intercept**.

The point at which the line passes through the y-axis is called the **y-intercept**.

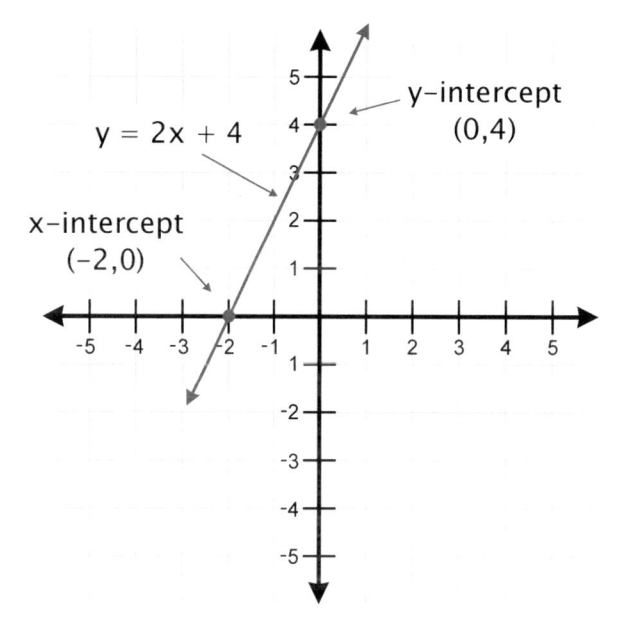

To draw the line represented by the equation:
1. Find some points: Choose values for x to be the x-coordinates, then plug those values into the equation to find the corresponding y-coordinates.
2. Draw a line connecting the points.

Example: Sketch the graph of the linear equation y = 3x + 1.

First, choose some x-coordinate values. Then substitute those values into the equation to figure out the corresponding y-coordinates.

Using the equation y = 3x + 1:

x=0
y = 3x + 1
y = 3(0) + 1   *substituting x = 0*
y = 1   point: (0,1)

x=1
y = 3x + 1
y = 3(1) + 1   *substituting x = 1*
y = 4   point: (1,4)

x=-1
y = 3x + 1
y = 3(-1) + 1   *substituting x = -1*
y = -2   point: (-1,-2)

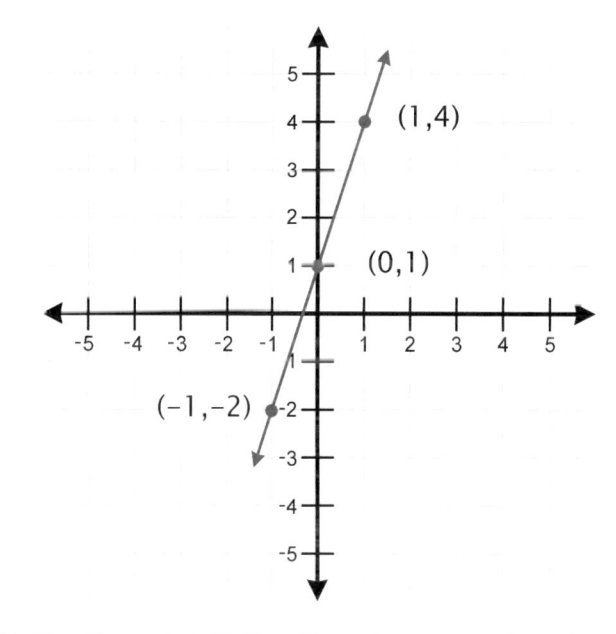

Notice the point (0,1) is the y-intercept since it is the point where the line passes through the y-axis. At this point x = 0.

Next, connect the points by drawing a straight line joining them.

In the previous example, x-coordinate values were chosen in order to find the corresponding y-coordinate values. When x was set to 0, the point was on the y-axis. This is the **y-intercept**.

> The **y-intercept** is the point at which the x-coordinate is 0 (it's on the y-axis).
>   Set x=0 and solve the equation for **y**.
>
> The **x-intercept** is the point at which the y-coordinate is 0 (it's on the x-axis).
>   Set y=0 and solve the equation for **x**.

Example: Find the x and y intercepts of the linear equation y = 4x + 2 and draw its graph.

y-intercept
The y-intercept is the point at which x = 0.

Using the equation y = 4x + 2 with x=0:
y = 4x + 2
y = 4(0) + 2   *substituting x=0 and solving for y*
y = 2   point: (0,2)

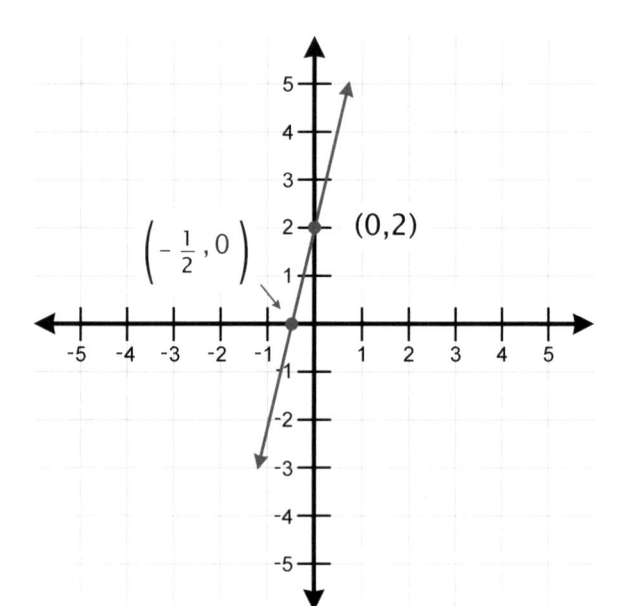

x-intercept
The x-intercept is the point at which y = 0.

The x-coordinate is found by using substitution with y=0 and solving for x.

Using the equation y = 4x + 2 with y=0:
y = 4x + 2
0 = 4x + 2   *substituting y=0 and solving for x*
0 − 2 = 4x
−2 = 4x

$-\dfrac{2}{4} = x$

$-\dfrac{1}{2} = x$ point: $\left(-\dfrac{1}{2}, 0\right)$

Only two points are needed to draw a straight line, so we can draw the line connecting the two intercepts.

Name _____ Date _____

Linear Equations and Intercepts

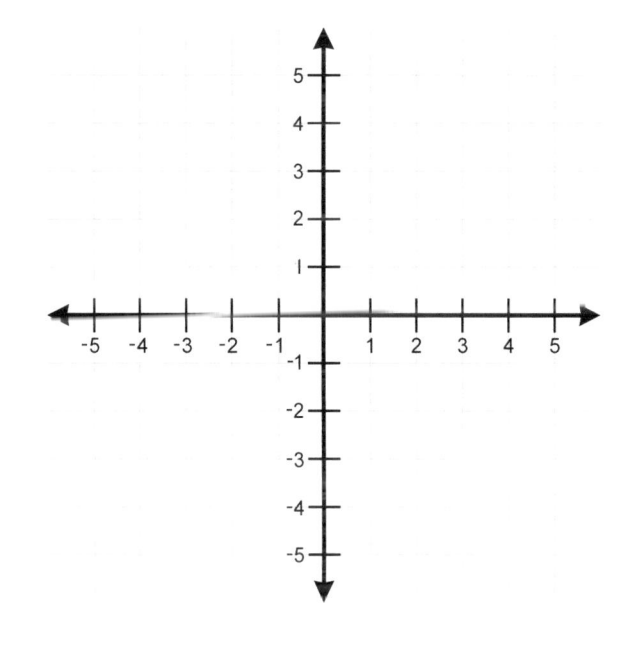

Graph and label the lines, and find their x and y intercepts.

Line A: y = x + 4

x-intercept: _____

y-intercept: _____

Line B: y = x − 5

x-intercept: _____

y-intercept: _____

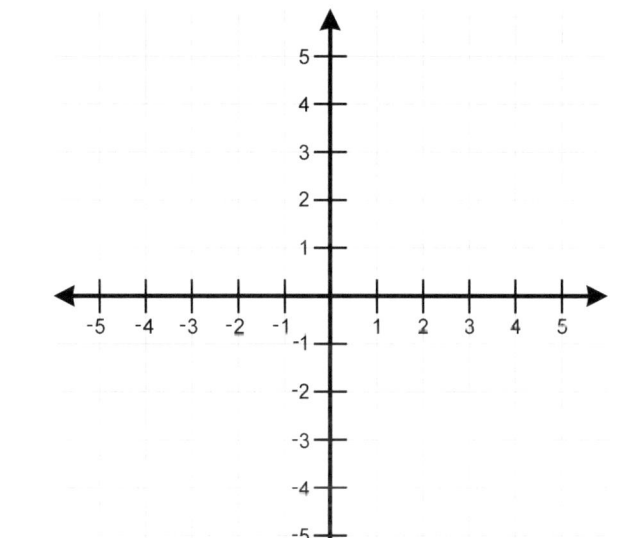

Line C: y = 3x + 3

x-intercept: _____

y-intercept: _____

Line D: y = $\frac{1}{2}$ x − 2

x-intercept: _____

y-intercept: _____

145   ClayMaze.com

Name _____   Date _____

Linear Equations and Intercepts

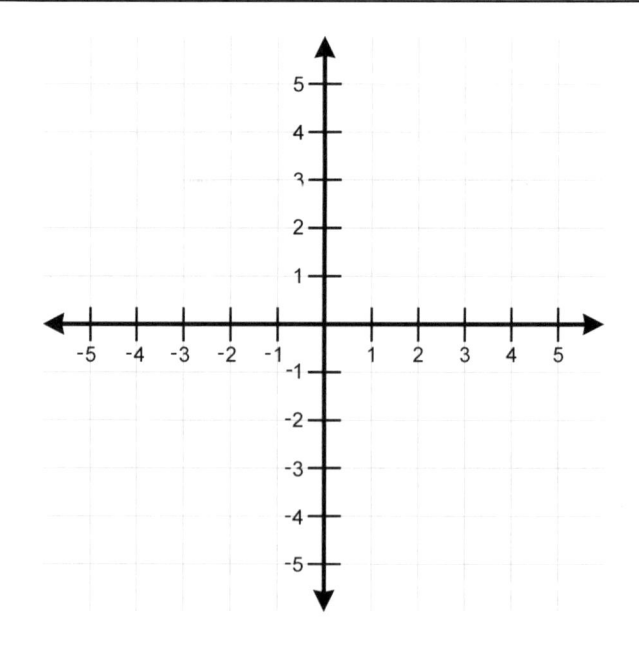

Graph and label the lines, and find their x and y intercepts.

Line A: $y = -x + 5$

x-intercept: _____

y-intercept: _____

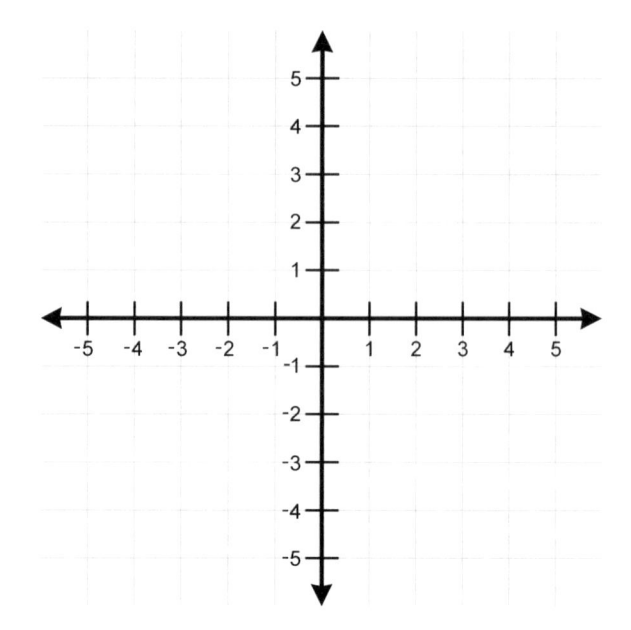

Line B: $y = x - 1$

x-intercept: _____

y-intercept: _____

Line C: $y = -2x + 4$

x-intercept: _____

y-intercept: _____

Line D: $y = 2x - 4$

x-intercept: _____

y-intercept: _____

Name _____   Date _____

Linear Equations and Intercepts

Graph and label the lines, and find their x and y intercepts.

Line A: y = x − 2

x-intercept: _____

y-intercept: _____

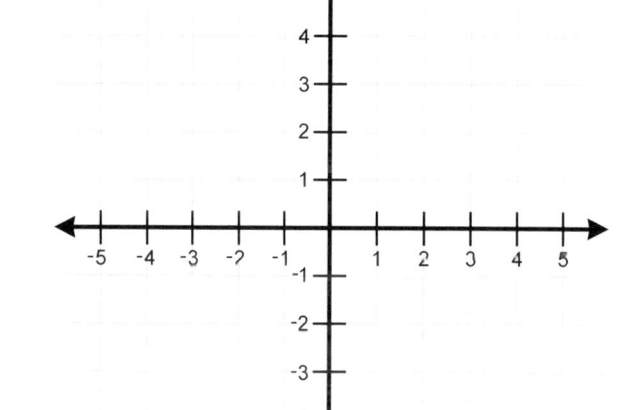

Line B: y = −x + 3

x-intercept: _____

y-intercept: _____

Line C: y = 5x − 5

x-intercept: _____

y-intercept: _____

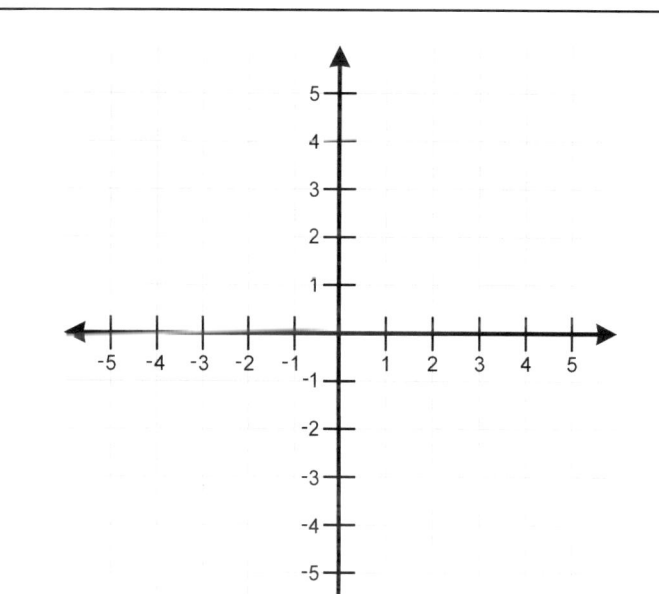

Line D: $y = \frac{1}{3}x + 1$

x-intercept: _____

y-intercept: _____

147   ClayMaze.com

Name _____   Date _____

Linear Equations and Intercepts

Graph and label the lines, and find their x and y intercepts.

Line A: $y = -x + 1$

x-intercept: _____

y-intercept: _____

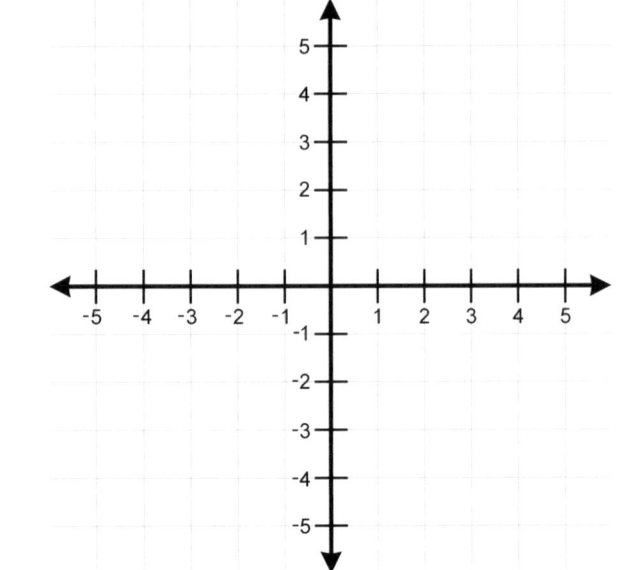

Line B: $y = 4x + 4$

x-intercept: _____

y-intercept: _____

Line C: $y = -\frac{1}{4}x + 1$

x-intercept: _____

y-intercept: _____

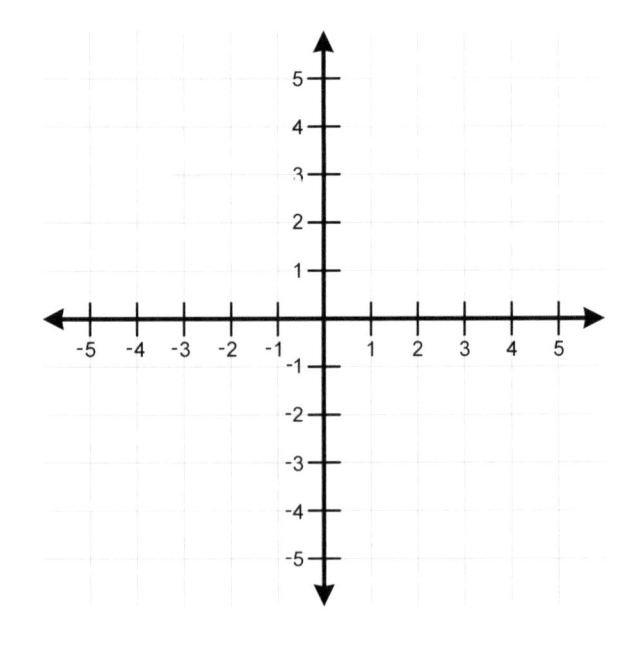

Line D: $y = -x - 2$

x-intercept: _____

y-intercept: _____

Slope-Intercept Form of the Line

The linear equations in the last section were in a form called the **slope-intercept form**, which looks like this:

$y = mx + b$, where m is the slope and (0,b) is the y-intercept.

Example: Find the slope and y-intercept of the lines. *(The equations of the lines are in the slope-intercept form: y = mx + b)*

a. $y = 5x + 8$ slope: __5__   y-intercept: __(0,8)__

b. $y = -\frac{1}{2}x + 3$ slope: __$-\frac{1}{2}$__   y-intercept: __(0,3)__

c. $y = 7x - 4$ slope: __7__   y-intercept: __(0,-4)__

Example: Find the equations of the lines for the given slopes and y-intercepts.

a. slope: −5   y-intercept: (0,1)   Equation: __$y = -5x + 1$__

b. slope: $\frac{3}{4}$ y-intercept: (0,−6)   Equation: __$y = \frac{3}{4}x - 6$__

Example: Find the slope-intercept equation (y = mx + b) of the line shown below.

Using the graph to the right, the formula of the line can be determined in a few steps:

1. Find the y-intercept.

    This is the point (0,1), so b = 1

2. Choose another point on the line to get the slope.

    Another point this line passes through is (2,5).

    Slope of the line through (0,1) and (2,5):

    $m = \frac{5-1}{2-0} = \frac{4}{2} = 2$ m = 2

3. Plug in the values for slope and intercept.

    $y = 2x + 1$

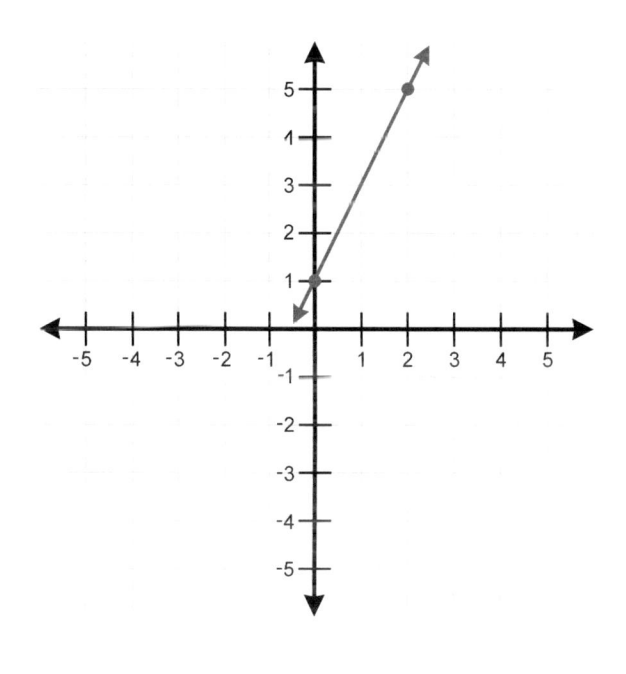

Example: Find the slope and y-intercept of the equations and draw their graphs.

a. $y = \dfrac{2}{3}x - 4$

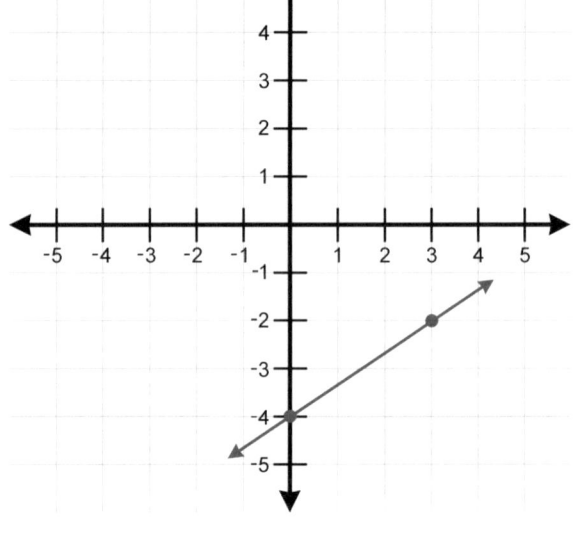

First, plot the y-intercept.

  Looking at the equation, we can see that the slope is $\dfrac{2}{3}$ and the y-intercept is $(0,-4)$.

Next, using the slope we can plot another point.

  Since the slope is $\dfrac{2}{3}$,

  the rise is 2 and the run is 3.

  Starting from the y-intercept point, count 2 units up and 3 units to the right then mark this point.

  The line can now be drawn passing through the y-intercept and the new point.

b. $y = -3x + 5$

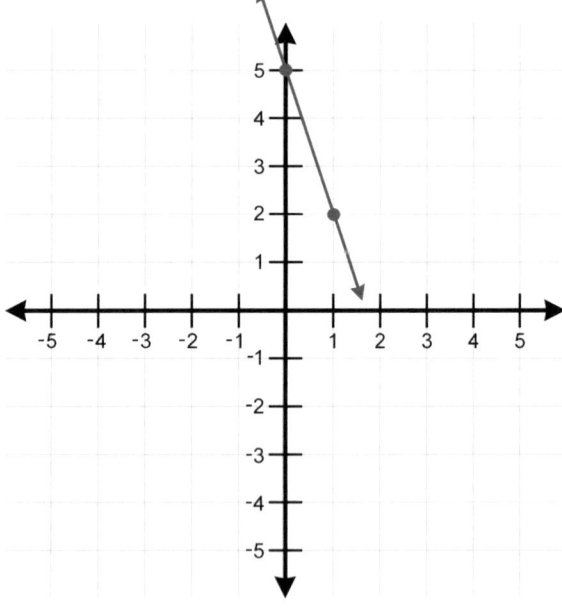

First, plot the y-intercept.

  Looking at the equation, we can see that the slope is -3 and the y-intercept is $(0,5)$.

Next, using the slope we can plot another point.

  Since the slope is -3, we know that the slope is downward. -3 can be either $\dfrac{-3}{1}$ or $\dfrac{3}{-1}$ to represent $\dfrac{rise}{run}$, so either one can be chosen.

Using $\dfrac{-3}{1}$, rise = -3 (down 3 units) and run = 1 (1 unit to the right).

This gives the point $(1,2)$, and the line can be drawn passing through that point and the y-intercept.

Name _____   Date _____

Slope-Intercept Equations

Find the y-intercept and slope of each line.

1. Line: $y = 4x + 5$

   y-intercept: _____   slope: _____

2. Line: $y = 8x - 3$

   y-intercept: _____   slope: _____

3. Line: $y = -x + 12$

   y-intercept: _____   slope: _____

4. Line: $y = \frac{2}{3}x + 7$

   y-intercept: _____   slope: _____

5. Line: $y = \frac{5}{2}x + 3$

   y-intercept: _____   slope: _____

6. Line: $y = -6x - 1$

   y-intercept: _____   slope: _____

7. Line: $y = -4x - 1$

   y-intercept: _____   slope: _____

8. Line: $y = 3x + 5$

   y-intercept: _____   slope: _____

9. Line: $y = \frac{1}{3}x - 2$

   y-intercept: _____   slope: _____

10. Line: $y = \frac{7}{4}x + 3$

    y-intercept: _____   slope: _____

Find the equations of the lines given their y-intercept and slope.

1. y-intercept: (0,8)   slope: 1

   Line:

2. y-intercept: (0,-3)   slope: 10

   Line:

3. y-intercept: (0,-1)   slope: 4

   Line:

4. y-intercept: (0,4)   slope: $-\frac{5}{2}$

   Line:

5. y-intercept: (0,3)   slope: $\frac{1}{2}$

   Line:

6. y-intercept: (0,-7)   slope: -1

   Line:

7. y-intercept: (0,-4)   slope: 11

   Line:

8. y-intercept: (0,2)   slope: 7

   Line:

9. y-intercept: (0,-2)   slope: $\frac{1}{4}$

   Line:

10. y-intercept: (0,1)   slope: $\frac{5}{6}$

    Line:

Name _____   Date _____

Slope-Intercept Equations

Find the slope-intercept equation (y = mx + b) of the lines shown.

Line A:

y-intercept: _____   slope: _____

line:

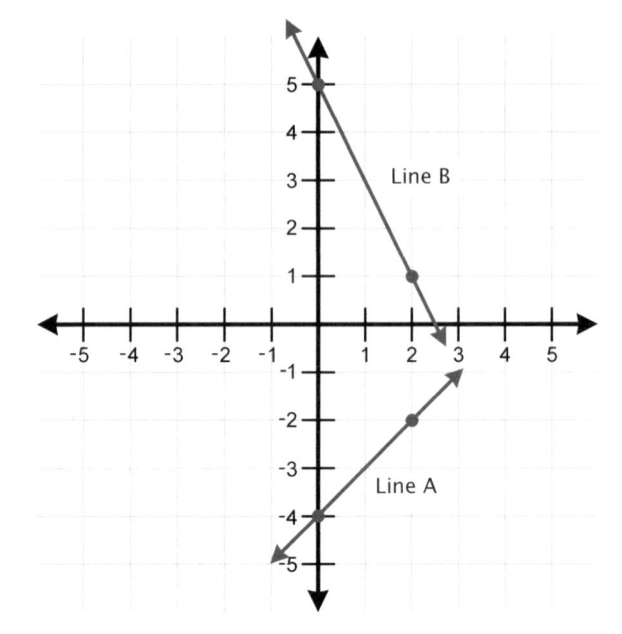

Line B:

y-intercept: _____   slope: _____

line:

Line C:

y-intercept: _____   slope: _____

line:

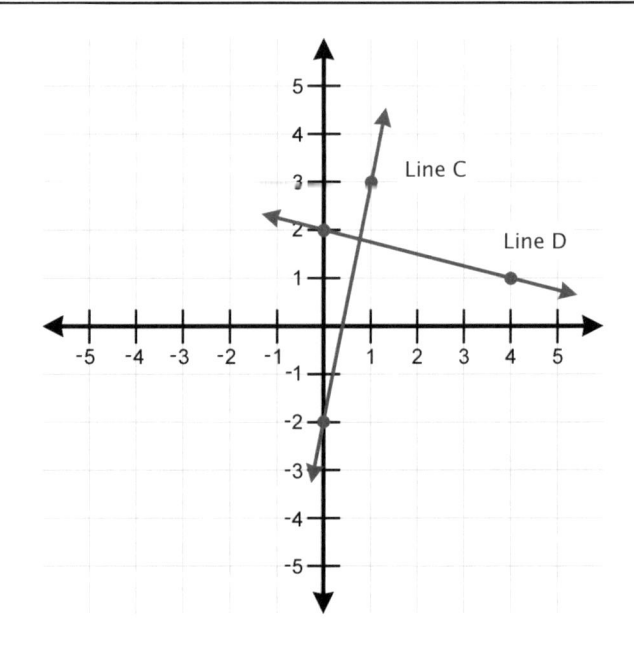

Line D:

y-intercept: _____   slope: _____

line:

152   ClayMaze.com

Name _____ Date _____

Slope-Intercept Equations

Find the y-intercept and slope of the given lines and draw their graphs.

Line A: y = 2x − 3

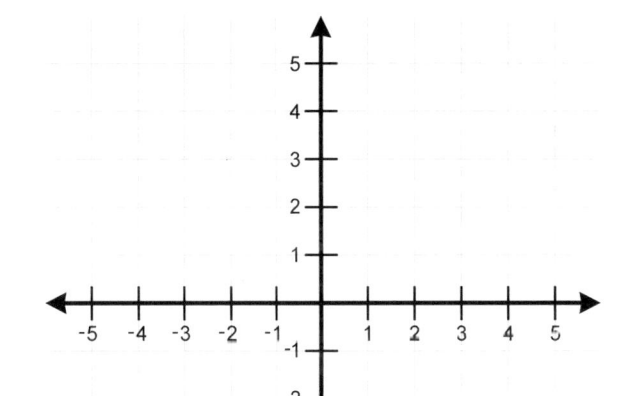

y-intercept: _____   slope: _____

Line B: y = −3x + 4

y-intercept: _____   slope: _____

Line C: y = 4x + 1

y-intercept: _____   slope: _____

Line D: $y = -\frac{1}{5}x - 4$

y-intercept: _____   slope: _____

Line E: y = 4x − 3

y-intercept: _____   slope: _____

Line F: $y = \frac{2}{5}x + 1$

y-intercept: _____   slope: _____

---

153   ClayMaze.com

Name _____   Date _____

Slope-Intercept Equations

Find the y-intercept and slope of the given lines and draw their graphs.

Line A: $y = 3x + 1$

y-intercept: _____   slope: _____

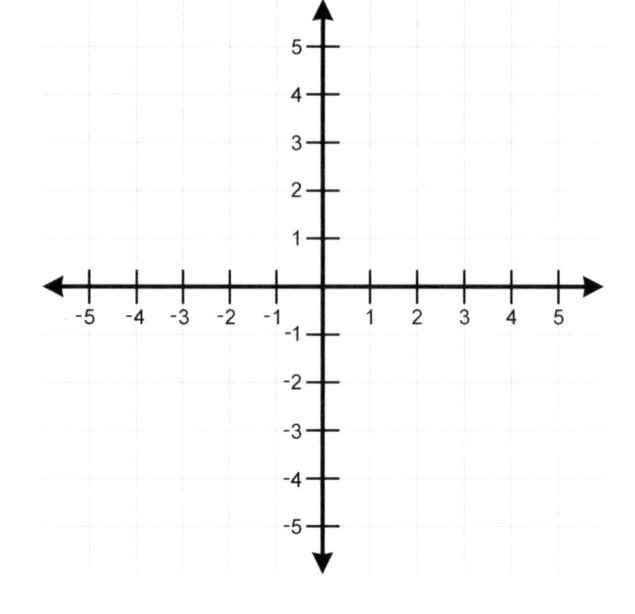

Line B: $y = -x - 2$

y-intercept: _____   slope: _____

Line C: $y = \frac{1}{4}x + 3$

y-intercept: _____   slope: _____

Line D: $y = -\frac{3}{2}x + 4$

y-intercept: _____   slope: _____

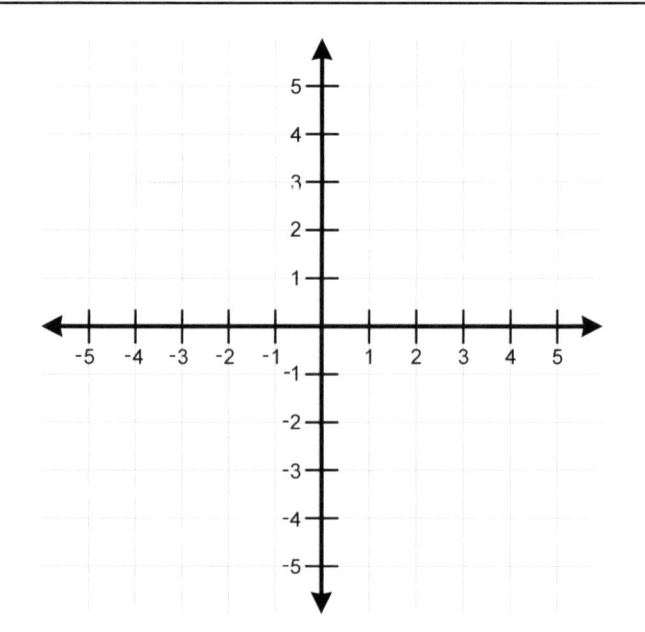

Line E: $y = 2x + 3$

y-intercept: _____   slope: _____

Line F: $y = 4x - 5$

y-intercept: _____   slope: _____

Solutions

Solutions to Problems

Negative Numbers

Fill in the blanks on the number lines with the missing numbers.

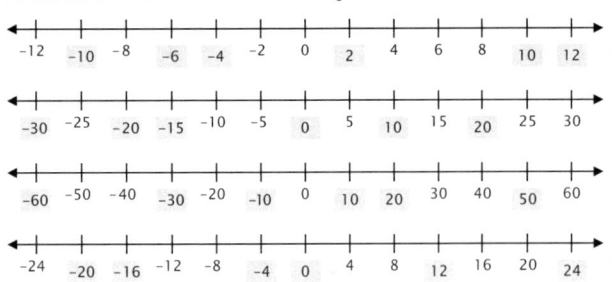

-12, -10, -8, -6, -4, -2, 0, 2, 4, 6, 8, 10, 12

-30, -25, -20, -15, -10, -5, 0, 5, 10, 15, 20, 25, 30

-60, -50, -40, -30, -20, -10, 0, 10, 20, 30, 40, 50, 60

-24, -20, -16, -12, -8, -4, 0, 4, 8, 12, 16, 20, 24

Compare the numbers in each pair and fill in the blanks with < or >.

1. -2 < 0
2. -12 < 11
3. 200 > -400
4. 50 > -52
5. -14 < -13
6. 29 > -35
7. -85 > -96
8. 27 > -84
9. -112 < -55
10. 4 > -7
11. 0 > -1
12. -34 > -35

Order the numbers in the sets from least to greatest.

1. {5, 6, -7, -3, 10, -12, 0}   {-12, -7, -3, 0, 5, 6, 10}
2. {12, -19, 13, -12, 15, 3, -7}   {-19, -12, -7, 3, 12, 13, 15}
3. {300, 0, -200, -500, 400, 800, 700}   {-500, -200, 0, 300, 400, 700, 800}
4. {-44, 40, -65, -21, 80, -40, -62}   {-65, -62, -44, -40, -21, 40, 80}

PAGE 2

Adding and Subtracting with Positive and Negative Numbers

Evaluate (Addition).

1. 3 + -57   -54
2. 53 + -2   51
3. 1 + -99   -98
4. 13 + -2   11
5. 14 + -2   12
6. 98 + -6   92
7. -2 + 8   6
8. 5 + -45   -40
9. 1 + -39   -38
10. -2 + -8   -10
11. 10 + -1   9
12. 8 + -28   -20
13. -17 + -6   -23
14. -93 + -1   -94
15. -19 + -6   -25
16. -6 + -98   -104
17. 17 + -6   11
18. 5 + -75   -70
19. 18 + -6   12
20. 6 + -89   -83
21. 9 + -29   -20

Evaluate (Subtraction).

1. -15 - 4   -19
2. 95 - -5   100
3. 52 - -1   53
4. -7 - 8   -15
5. -10 - 5   -15
6. 48 - 6   42
7. 13 - -4   17
8. 68 - -6   74
9. 5 - -45   50
10. 10 - 5   5
11. 12 - 2   10
12. 0 - -2   2
13. -20 - -1   -19
14. 2 - 28   -26
15. 6 - 20   -14
16. 15 - -3   18
17. -7 - 17   -24
18. -11 - 5   -16
19. 59 - -6   65
20. 19 - -6   25
21. -2 - -58   56

Evaluate (Mixed).

1. 1 + -9   -8
2. 9 - -9   18
3. 6 - -36   42
4. -9 - 59   -68
5. -3 - 77   -80
6. -5 + 65   60
7. 14 + -3   11
8. 3 + -47   -44
9. 12 - -2   14
10. -16 + 6   -10
11. -15 - 2   -17
12. 2 + -28   -26
13. 23 - 3   20
14. 20 + 1   21
15. 11 + -1   10
16. -41 - -1   -40
17. 6 - -57   63
18. 7 - -18   25
19. 45 + 4   49
20. -12 + 0   -12
21. 4 - -66   70

PAGE 4

Adding and Subtracting with Positive and Negative Numbers

Evaluate (Addition).

1. 10 + -2   8
2. 3 + -27   -24
3. 6 + -8   -2
4. 16 + -6   10
5. -25 + -2   -27
6. -6 + -39   -45
7. -7 + 77   70
8. -13 + -2   -15
9. -10 + -1   -11
10. -3 + 7   4
11. 20 + -5   15
12. 17 + -7   10
13. -15 + 0   -15
14. -3 + 57   54
15. 58 + -6   52
16. 87 + -6   81
17. -26 + 5   -21
18. 0 + -4   -4
19. -64 + 0   -64
20. 9 + -69   -60
21. 19 + -6   13

Evaluate (Subtraction).

1. 12 - 15   -3
2. 8 - 28   -20
3. -3 - 17   -20
4. 0 - 4   -4
5. 11 - 0   11
6. -58 - -6   -52
7. -12 - 1   -13
8. 58 - -4   62
9. 1 - 59   -58
10. 14 - -5   19
11. -11 - -1   -10
12. 13 - 3   10
13. 3 - -47   50
14. 10 - -4   14
15. 7 - 98   -91
16. 15 - -2   17
17. 7 - -9   16
18. 11 - -1   12
19. 16 - -6   22
20. -3 - -67   64
21. 29 - -5   34

Evaluate (Mixed).

1. -6 + 8   2
2. 13 - -2   15
3. 4 - -96   100
4. -23 + 2   -21
5. 28 - -1   29
6. 82 - -7   89
7. -44 + 0   -44
8. -3 + -7   -10
9. -5 - 55   -60
10. -83 - -3   -80
11. -18 + 6   -12
12. -1 - 29   -30
13. -13 + 1   -12
14. 6 + -49   -43
15. 2 + -64   -62
16. -1 + 79   78
17. -8 - 19   -27
18. -15 - 4   -19
19. 19 - -6   25
20. -10 + -4   -14
21. -3 + 27   24

PAGE 5

Multiplying and Dividing with Positive and Negative Numbers

Multiply.

1. -4 x -7   28
2. -9 x -12   108
3. 7 x 8   56
4. -6 x -11   66
5. 8 x 12   96
6. 4 x 10   40
7. -7 x -2   14
8. -6 x -6   36
9. -5 x -11   55
10. -6 x 12   -72
11. 11 x -2   -22
12. 7 x -4   -28
13. -9 x 11   -99
14. 5 x -7   -35
15. -10 x -6   60
16. 3 x -4   -12
17. -7 x 1   -7
18. -12 x 8   -96
19. -12 x -2   24
20. -7 x -2   11
21. 7 x -5   35
22. -9 x -3   27
23. 9 x -5   -45
24. 4 x -7   -28
25. -5 x -1 x -2   -10
26. -6 x -4 x -1   -24
27. 10 x -4 x -3   120
28. -8 x -5 x -4   -160
29. -7 x 3 x -2   42
30. -5 x -11 x -2   -110

Divide.

1. 8 ÷ 2   4
2. 96 ÷ -8   -12
3. 48 ÷ -8   -6
4. -22 ÷ -2   11
5. 5 ÷ -1   -5
6. -20 ÷ -4   5
7. -15 ÷ -5   3
8. -63 ÷ 9   -7
9. -54 ÷ -9   6
10. 5 ÷ -5   -1
11. -88 ÷ 11   -8
12. 4 ÷ -2   -2
13. -16 ÷ -2   8
14. -18 ÷ -9   2
15. 28 ÷ -7   -4
16. -45 ÷ -5   9
17. 36 ÷ -12   -3
18. -48 ÷ -6   8
19. -64 ÷ -8   8
20. 2 ÷ -2   -1
21. -90 ÷ -9   10
22. 110 ÷ -11   -10
23. -40 ÷ -5   8
24. 132 ÷ -11   -12
25. 27 ÷ -3   -9
26. 24 ÷ -4   -6
27. -8 ÷ -4   2
28. -33 ÷ -3   11
29. 9 ÷ -3   -3
30. 108 ÷ -12   -9
31. 24 ÷ -3   -8
32. 70 ÷ -10   -7
33. -3 ÷ -1   3

PAGE 7

Multiplying and Dividing with Positive and Negative Numbers

Multiply.

1. -2 × 5 = **-10**
2. -10 × -8 = **80**
3. -3 × 11 = **-33**
4. 12 × -10 = **-120**
5. -4 × -5 = **20**
6. 2 × -6 = **-12**
7. -2 × -11 = **22**
8. -5 × 6 = **-30**
9. -12 × -12 = **144**
10. 2 × -8 = **-16**
11. 12 × -2 = **-24**
12. -5 × 12 = **-60**
13. -8 × 7 = **-56**
14. -8 × -2 = **16**
15. -2 × -2 = **4**
16. -10 × -9 = **90**
17. -10 × -10 = **100**
18. -7 × -7 = **49**
19. 3 × -10 = **-30**
20. 5 × -11 = **-55**
21. -3 × -12 = **36**
22. -5 × 5 = **-25**
23. -7 × -3 = **21**
24. -2 × 4 = **-8**
25. 6 × -7 × -1 = **42**
26. 10 × -9 × -1 = **90**
27. -2 × -5 × -3 = **-30**
28. -3 × -4 × 2 = **24**
29. -7 × 5 × 2 = **-70**
30. -11 × -2 × -4 = **-88**

Divide.

1. -30 ÷ 6 = **-5**
2. -50 ÷ 10 = **-5**
3. 24 ÷ -6 = **-4**
4. 72 ÷ -8 = **-9**
5. -12 ÷ -2 = **6**
6. -12 ÷ -6 = **2**
7. -77 ÷ -7 = **11**
8. -84 ÷ -7 = **12**
9. -42 ÷ -7 = **6**
10. 120 ÷ -12 = **-10**
11. -7 ÷ -1 = **7**
12. 50 ÷ -5 = **-10**
13. -16 ÷ 2 = **-8**
14. 10 ÷ -5 = **-2**
15. 6 ÷ -2 = **-3**
16. -22 ÷ -11 = **2**
17. -60 ÷ 12 = **-5**
18. -48 ÷ -12 = **4**
19. -21 ÷ 3 = **-7**
20. -27 ÷ 9 = **-3**
21. 12 ÷ -3 = **-4**
22. -4 ÷ 2 = **-2**
23. -24 ÷ -12 = **2**
24. -14 ÷ 2 = **-7**
25. -32 ÷ 4 = **-8**
26. -44 ÷ 4 = **-11**
27. -25 ÷ -5 = **5**
28. -15 ÷ -3 = **5**
29. 64 ÷ -8 = **-8**
30. -20 ÷ -2 = **10**
31. -28 ÷ -7 = **4**
32. -12 ÷ -4 = **3**
33. 18 ÷ -9 = **-2**

PAGE 8

Exponents

Fill in the blanks using the appropriate form (word form, exponential form or expanded form):

	Word Form	Exponential Form	Expanded Form
1.	seven squared	7^2	7 × 7
2.	thirteen to the first power	13^1	13
3.	three to the fifth power	3^5	3 × 3 × 3 × 3 × 3
4.	five to the seventh power	5^7	5 × 5 × 5 × 5 × 5 × 5 × 5
5.	eleven to the fifth power	11^5	11 × 11 × 11 × 11 × 11
6.	eight to the eighth power	8^8	8 × 8 × 8 × 8 × 8 × 8 × 8 × 8
7.	fifteen cubed (or to the 3rd power)	15^3	15 × 15 × 15
8.	four to the sixth power	4^6	4 × 4 × 4 × 4 × 4 × 4

The word form may vary. For example, "sixty-five to the fourth power" could also be written as "sixty-five to the power of 4".

Evaluate.

1. 3^2 = **9**
2. 6^4 = **1,296**
3. 2^0 = **1**
4. 0^5 = **0**
5. 12^3 = **1,728**
6. 12^1 = **12**
7. $(-3)^4$ = **81**
8. 20^2 = **400**
9. 1^5 = **1**
10. $(-4)^5$ = **-1,024**
11. 9^2 = **81**
12. $(-11)^3$ = **-1,331**
13. 0^3 = **0**
14. 78^0 = **1**
15. 16^1 = **16**
16. 32^2 = **1,024**
17. 200^2 = **40,000**
18. 16^2 = **256**

PAGE 11

Exponents

Fill in the blanks using the appropriate form (word form, exponential form or expanded form):

	Word Form	Exponential Form	Expanded Form
1.	three to the seventh power	3^7	3 × 3 × 3 × 3 × 3 × 3 × 3
2.	forty-four squared	44^2	44 × 44
3.	five to the fifth power	5^5	5 × 5 × 5 × 5 × 5
4.	one hundred to the fourth power	100^4	100 × 100 × 100 × 100
5.	fourteen cubed	14^3	14 × 14 × 14
6.	twelve to the fifth power	12^5	12 × 12 × 12 × 12 × 12
7.	sixty-five to the fourth power	65^4	65 × 65 × 65 × 65
8.	twenty-four squared	24^2	24 × 24

The word form may vary. For example, "twelve to the fifth power" could also be written as "twelve to the power of 5".

Evaluate.

1. 8^1 = **8**
2. 17^2 = **289**
3. 25^0 = **1**
4. 13^2 = **169**
5. $(-3)^5$ = **-243**
6. 9^4 = **6,561**
7. 5^4 = **625**
8. 50^2 = **2,500**
9. 64^1 = **64**
10. 3^0 = **1**
11. 0^6 = **0**
12. 2^6 = **64**
13. $(-10)^4$ = **10,000**
14. 300^2 = **90,000**
15. 2^7 = **128**
16. 8^3 = **512**
17. 12^4 = **20,736**
18. $(-40)^2$ = **1,600**

PAGE 12

Negative Exponents

Evaluate.

1. 8^{-1} = $\dfrac{1}{8}$
2. 3^{-5} = $\dfrac{1}{243}$
3. $(-7)^{-2}$ = $\dfrac{1}{49}$
4. 2^{-6} = $\dfrac{1}{64}$
5. $(-4)^{-3}$ = $-\dfrac{1}{64}$
6. 3^{-4} = $\dfrac{1}{81}$
7. 11^{-2} = $\dfrac{1}{121}$
8. $\left(\dfrac{1}{5}\right)^{-5}$ = **3,125**
9. $\left(\dfrac{1}{2}\right)^{-4}$ = **16**
10. $\left(\dfrac{1}{7}\right)^{-3}$ = **343**

PAGE 15

157 ClayMaze.com

Negative Exponents

Evaluate.

1. 10^{-3}

    $\dfrac{1}{1,000}$

2. $(-8)^{-2}$

    $\dfrac{1}{64}$

3. $(-2)^{-5}$

    $-\dfrac{1}{32}$

4. 3^{-1}

    $\dfrac{1}{3}$

5. 7^{-4}

    $\dfrac{1}{2,401}$

6. 16^{-2}

    $\dfrac{1}{256}$

7. 5^{-4}

    $\dfrac{1}{625}$

8. $(-1)^{-5}$

    -1

9. $\left(\dfrac{1}{10}\right)^{-4}$

    $10,000$

10. $\left(\dfrac{1}{11}\right)^{-1}$

    11

PAGE 16

Roots

Evaluate.

1. $\sqrt{4}$ — 2
2. $\sqrt{64}$ — 8
3. $\sqrt{25}$ — 5
4. $\sqrt{16}$ — 4
5. $\sqrt{81}$ — 9
6. $\sqrt{121}$ — 11
7. $\sqrt{144}$ — 12
8. $\sqrt{1}$ — 1
9. $\sqrt{49}$ — 7
10. $\sqrt{100}$ — 10
11. $\sqrt{36}$ — 6
12. $\sqrt{0}$ — 0
13. $\sqrt{400}$ — 20
14. $\sqrt{900}$ — 30
15. $\sqrt[3]{8}$ — 2
16. $\sqrt[3]{-1}$ — -1
17. $\sqrt[3]{64}$ — 4
18. $\sqrt[3]{-125}$ — -5
19. $\sqrt[3]{-27}$ — -3
20. $\sqrt[3]{1,000}$ — 10

PAGE 18

Divisibility Rules & Factors

Circle the grey numbers that divide evenly into the given numbers in the left column.

1. 14 — ②, 3, 4, 5, 6, ⑦, 8, 9, 10
2. 135 — 2, ③, 4, ⑤, 6, 7, 8, ⑨, 10
3. 306 — ②, ③, 4, 5, ⑥, 7, 8, ⑨, 10
4. 1,620 — ②, ③, ④, ⑤, ⑥, 7, 8, ⑨, ⑩
5. 4,002 — ②, ③, 4, 5, 6, 7, 8, 9, 10
6. 25,238 — ②, 3, 4, 5, 6, 7, 8, 9, 10

List the factors of the numbers below. If a given number is prime, write prime.

7. 12 — 1, 2, 3, 4, 6, 12
8. 64 — 1, 2, 4, 8, 16, 32, 64
9. 51 — 1, 3, 17, 51
10. 65 — 1, 5, 13, 65
11. 121 — 1, 11, 121
12. 70 — 1, 2, 5, 7, 10, 14, 35, 70
13. 32 — 1, 2, 4, 8, 16, 32
14. 47 — 1, 47   prime

PAGE 21

Divisibility Rules & Factors

Circle the grey numbers that divide evenly into the given numbers in the left column.

1. 45 — 2, ③, 4, ⑤, 6, 7, 8, ⑨, 10
2. 175 — 2, 3, 4, ⑤, 6, ⑦, 8, 9, 10
3. 316 — ②, 3, ④, 5, 6, 7, 8, 9, 10
4. 1,744 — ②, 3, ④, 5, 6, 7, ⑧, 9, 10
5. 5,420 — ②, 3, ④, ⑤, 6, 7, 8, 9, ⑩
6. 45,950 — ②, 3, 4, ⑤, 6, 7, 8, 9, ⑩

List the factors of the numbers below. If a given number is prime, write prime.

7. 9 — 1, 3, 9
8. 54 — 1, 2, 3, 6, 9, 18, 27, 54
9. 60 — 1, 2, 3, 4, 5, 6, 10, 12, 15, 20, 30, 60
10. 36 — 1, 2, 3, 4, 6, 9, 12, 18, 36
11. 29 — 1, 29   prime
12. 15 — 1, 3, 5, 15
13. 125 — 1, 5, 25, 125
14. 100 — 1, 2, 4, 5, 10, 20, 25, 50, 100

PAGE 22

Prime Factorization

Write the prime factorization of the following numbers in the blanks below.

1. 12

   $2^2 \times 3$

2. 24

   $2^3 \times 3$

3. 25

   5^2

4. 75

   3×5^2

5. 64

   2^6

6. 21

   3×7

7. 51

   3×17

8. 100

   $2^2 \times 5^2$

9. 57

   3×19

10. 120

    $2^3 \times 3 \times 5$

11. 84

    $2^2 \times 3 \times 7$

12. 125

    5^3

PAGE 24

Greatest Common Factor (GCF)

Find the GCF.

1. 16, 18   GCF: 2
2. 35, 21   GCF: 7
3. 24, 36   GCF: 12
4. 54, 36   GCF: 18
5. 10, 55   GCF: 5
6. 21, 27   GCF: 3
7. 54, 25   GCF: 1
8. 56, 120   GCF: 8
9. 70, 140   GCF: 70
10. 42, 30   GCF: 6
11. 24, 12, 45   GCF: 3
12. 60, 24, 36   GCF: 12

PAGE 26

Greatest Common Factor (GCF)

Find the GCF.

1. 20, 24   GCF: 4
2. 12, 8   GCF: 4
3. 45, 30   GCF: 15
4. 25, 75   GCF: 25
5. 13, 26   GCF: 13
6. 121, 77   GCF: 11
7. 24, 90   GCF: 6
8. 33, 15   GCF: 3
9. 56, 49   GCF: 7
10. 39, 24   GCF: 3
11. 8, 48, 16   GCF: 8
12. 60, 120, 85   GCF: 5

PAGE 27

Least Common Multiple (LCM)

Find the LCM.

1. 6, 12   LCM: 12
2. 4, 6   LCM: 12
3. 3, 7   LCM: 21
4. 5, 20   LCM: 20
5. 8, 10   LCM: 40
6. 4, 50   LCM: 100
7. 30, 9   LCM: 90
8. 3, 4   LCM: 12
9. 12, 5   LCM: 60
10. 6, 15   LCM: 30
11. 12, 4, 8   LCM: 24
12. 5, 3, 6   LCM: 30

PAGE 29

159

Least Common Multiple (LCM)

Find the LCM.

1. 7, 2 — LCM: 14
2. 30, 12 — LCM: 60
3. 15, 45 — LCM: 45
4. 4, 10 — LCM: 20
5. 25, 3 — LCM: 75
6. 12, 18 — LCM: 36
7. 18, 36 — LCM: 36
8. 20, 6 — LCM: 60
9. 25, 4 — LCM: 100
10. 24, 36 — LCM: 72
11. 4, 5, 8 — LCM: 40
12. 6, 12, 20 — LCM: 60

PAGE 30

Equivalent Fractions

Fill in each blank with the missing numerator or denominator to make the fractions equivalent.

1. $\frac{6}{25} = \frac{12}{50}$
2. $\frac{8}{10} = \frac{72}{90}$
3. $\frac{4}{8} = \frac{20}{40}$
4. $\frac{4}{11} = \frac{28}{77}$
5. $\frac{8}{9} = \frac{16}{18}$
6. $\frac{9}{25} = \frac{18}{50}$
7. $\frac{7}{8} = \frac{56}{64}$
8. $\frac{8}{11} = \frac{56}{77}$
9. $\frac{8}{9} = \frac{64}{72}$
10. $\frac{6}{8} = \frac{30}{40}$
11. $\frac{7}{8} = \frac{21}{24}$
12. $\frac{6}{100} = \frac{18}{300}$
13. $\frac{9}{12} = \frac{27}{36}$
14. $\frac{5}{25} = \frac{15}{75}$
15. $\frac{8}{25} = \frac{32}{100}$
16. $\frac{6}{10} = \frac{24}{40}$
17. $\frac{5}{9} = \frac{25}{45}$
18. $\frac{4}{12} = \frac{16}{48}$
19. $\frac{7}{25} = \frac{28}{100}$
20. $\frac{8}{22} = \frac{32}{88}$
21. $\frac{9}{25} = \frac{36}{100}$
22. $\frac{4}{5} = \frac{12}{15}$
23. $\frac{9}{10} = \frac{54}{60}$
24. $\frac{8}{20} = \frac{24}{60}$
25. $\frac{5}{12} = \frac{15}{36}$
26. $\frac{5}{6} = \frac{35}{42}$
27. $\frac{4}{12} = \frac{16}{48}$
28. $\frac{4}{10} = \frac{20}{50}$
29. $\frac{4}{7} = \frac{20}{35}$
30. $\frac{5}{9} = \frac{25}{45}$

PAGE 32

Simplifying Fractions

Simplify the fractions.

1. $\frac{2}{6} = \frac{1}{3}$
2. $\frac{16}{20} = \frac{4}{5}$
3. $\frac{18}{75} = \frac{6}{25}$
4. $\frac{8}{100} = \frac{2}{25}$
5. $\frac{6}{12} = \frac{1}{2}$
6. $\frac{40}{55} = \frac{8}{11}$
7. $\frac{36}{45} = \frac{4}{5}$
8. $\frac{72}{80} = \frac{9}{10}$
9. $\frac{24}{30} = \frac{4}{5}$
10. $\frac{24}{28} = \frac{6}{7}$
11. $\frac{18}{50} = \frac{9}{25}$
12. $\frac{10}{25} = \frac{2}{5}$
13. $\frac{140}{200} = \frac{7}{10}$
14. $\frac{180}{360} = \frac{1}{2}$
15. $\frac{256}{512} = \frac{1}{2}$

PAGE 34

Improper Fractions & Mixed Numbers

Convert the improper fractions to mixed numbers.

1. $\frac{16}{7}$ — $2\frac{2}{7}$
2. $\frac{37}{5}$ — $7\frac{2}{5}$
3. $\frac{9}{2}$ — $4\frac{1}{2}$
4. $\frac{57}{23}$ — $2\frac{11}{23}$
5. $\frac{45}{11}$ — $4\frac{1}{11}$
6. $\frac{35}{6}$ — $5\frac{5}{6}$
7. $\frac{44}{5}$ — $8\frac{4}{5}$
8. $\frac{7}{2}$ — $3\frac{1}{2}$
9. $\frac{67}{8}$ — $8\frac{3}{8}$
10. $\frac{7}{5}$ — $1\frac{2}{5}$
11. $\frac{71}{8}$ — $8\frac{7}{8}$
12. $\frac{57}{41}$ — $1\frac{16}{41}$
13. $\frac{22}{3}$ — $7\frac{1}{3}$
14. $\frac{26}{7}$ — $3\frac{5}{7}$
15. $\frac{79}{15}$ — $5\frac{4}{15}$

PAGE 37

Improper Fractions & Mixed Numbers

Convert the mixed numbers to improper fractions.

1. $1\frac{4}{5}$ = $\frac{9}{5}$
2. $5\frac{5}{9}$ = $\frac{50}{9}$
3. $2\frac{3}{11}$ = $\frac{25}{11}$
4. $2\frac{9}{25}$ = $\frac{59}{25}$
5. $4\frac{4}{15}$ = $\frac{64}{15}$
6. $6\frac{2}{3}$ = $\frac{20}{3}$
7. $5\frac{7}{10}$ = $\frac{57}{10}$
8. $3\frac{3}{25}$ = $\frac{78}{25}$
9. $2\frac{3}{4}$ = $\frac{11}{4}$
10. $4\frac{3}{20}$ = $\frac{83}{20}$
11. $2\frac{5}{14}$ = $\frac{33}{14}$
12. $3\frac{5}{8}$ = $\frac{29}{8}$
13. $4\frac{5}{6}$ = $\frac{29}{6}$
14. $8\frac{3}{7}$ = $\frac{59}{7}$
15. $3\frac{7}{22}$ = $\frac{73}{22}$

PAGE 38

Adding and Subtracting Fractions

Add the fractions and simplify.

1. $\frac{1}{2} + \frac{3}{8}$ = $\frac{7}{8}$
2. $\frac{3}{7} + \frac{2}{3}$ = $1\frac{2}{21}$
3. $\frac{2}{5} + \frac{5}{6}$ = $1\frac{7}{30}$
4. $\frac{1}{2} + \frac{4}{5}$ = $1\frac{3}{10}$
5. $\frac{2}{3} + \frac{1}{5} + \frac{5}{6}$ = $1\frac{7}{10}$

Subtract the fractions and simplify.

6. $\frac{4}{5} - \frac{2}{3}$ = $\frac{2}{15}$
7. $\frac{1}{3} - \frac{3}{11}$ = $\frac{2}{33}$
8. $\frac{2}{3} - \frac{1}{6}$ = $\frac{1}{2}$
9. $\frac{3}{4} - \frac{5}{8}$ = $\frac{1}{8}$
10. $\frac{5}{12} - \frac{1}{8}$ = $\frac{7}{24}$

PAGE 41

Adding and Subtracting Fractions

Add the fractions and simplify.

1. $\frac{1}{2} + \frac{2}{5}$ = $\frac{9}{10}$
2. $\frac{2}{3} + \frac{2}{5}$ = $1\frac{1}{15}$
3. $\frac{1}{5} + \frac{3}{4}$ = $\frac{19}{20}$
4. $\frac{1}{4} + \frac{5}{6}$ = $1\frac{1}{12}$
5. $\frac{2}{5} + \frac{1}{2} + \frac{1}{10}$ = 1

Subtract the fractions and simplify.

6. $\frac{5}{6} - \frac{1}{3}$ = $\frac{1}{2}$
7. $\frac{3}{4} - \frac{1}{3}$ = $\frac{5}{12}$
8. $\frac{2}{3} - \frac{5}{9}$ = $\frac{1}{9}$
9. $\frac{5}{7} - \frac{2}{3}$ = $\frac{1}{21}$
10. $\frac{3}{4} - \frac{2}{5}$ = $\frac{7}{20}$

PAGE 42

Multiplying and Dividing Fractions

Multiply the fractions and simplify.

1. $\frac{2}{5} \times \frac{1}{3}$ = $\frac{2}{15}$
2. $\frac{3}{8} \times \frac{1}{2}$ = $\frac{3}{16}$
3. $\frac{9}{10} \times \frac{4}{10}$ = $\frac{9}{25}$
4. $\frac{4}{7} \times \frac{3}{8}$ = $\frac{3}{14}$
5. $\frac{1}{2} \times \frac{2}{3} \times \frac{5}{8}$ = $\frac{5}{24}$

Divide the fractions and simplify.

6. $\frac{3}{4} \div \frac{1}{2}$ = $1\frac{1}{2}$
7. $\frac{8}{11} \div 2$ = $\frac{4}{11}$
8. $\frac{5}{9} \div \frac{2}{3}$ = $\frac{5}{6}$
9. $\frac{2}{3} \div \frac{1}{6}$ = 4
10. $\frac{9}{10} \div \frac{2}{5}$ = $2\frac{1}{4}$

PAGE 45

Multiplying and Dividing Fractions

Multiply the fractions and simplify.

1. $\frac{1}{6} \times \frac{4}{7} = \frac{2}{21}$

2. $\frac{2}{5} \times \frac{3}{4} = \frac{3}{10}$

3. $\frac{2}{4} \times \frac{1}{3} = \frac{1}{6}$

4. $\frac{2}{9} \times 3 = \frac{2}{3}$

5. $\frac{1}{3} \times \frac{5}{6} \times \frac{9}{10} = \frac{1}{4}$

Divide the fractions and simplify.

6. $\frac{3}{5} \div \frac{4}{9} = 1\frac{7}{20}$

7. $\frac{4}{7} \div \frac{2}{3} = \frac{6}{7}$

8. $\frac{1}{2} \div \frac{1}{4} = 2$

9. $\frac{5}{8} \div \frac{2}{8} = 2\frac{1}{2}$

10. $\frac{6}{11} \div \frac{3}{7} = 1\frac{3}{11}$

PAGE 46

Decimals

Write in expanded form.

1. 2.537 $2 + .5 + .03 + .007$
2. 37.0215 $30 + 7 + .02 + .001 + .0005$
3. 418.0104 $400 + 10 + 8 + .01 + .0004$
4. 12.5239 $10 + 2 + .5 + .02 + .003 + .0009$
5. 53.674 $50 + 3 + .6 + .07 + .004$

Evaluate.

1. 43.746 $40 + 3 + .7 + .04 + .006$
2. 201.8502 $200 + 1 + .8 + .05 + .0002$
3. 9.70431 $9 + .7 + .004 + .0003 + .00001$
4. 711.04003 $700 + 10 + 1 + .04 + .00003$
5. 85.05027 $80 + 5 + .05 + .0002 + .00007$

Order the numbers from least to greatest.

1. .462, .75, 1.1, .602, .09, .8   .09, .462, .602, .75, .8, 1.1
2. .112, .099, 2.09, .873, 2.23, .41 .099, .112, .41, .873, 2.09, 2.23
3. .056, 2.01, .094, .87, 2.005, .946 .056, .094, .87, .946, 2.005, 2.01
4. .149, .322, .371, .192, .098, .243 .098, .149, .192, .243, .322, .371
5. .15, 1.5, .085, .009, 1.28, .083   .009, .083, .085, .15, 1.28, 1.5
6. .982, .003, .76, .984, .054, .0031 .003, .0031, .054, .76, .982, .984

PAGE 48

Powers of 10

Evaluate.

1. 10^8 100,000,000
2. 10^{11} 100,000,000,000
3. 10^{-6} .000001
4. 10^{-9} .000000001
5. 10^{12} 1,000,000,000,000

Write as powers of 10.

1. 10^6 1,000,000
2. 10^{-10} .0000000001
3. 10^9 1,000,000,000
4. 10^{-7} .0000001
5. 10^{-12} .000000000001

Evaluate.

1. $10^4 + 10^1 + 10^{-2} + 10^{-3}$ 10,010.011
2. $10^2 + 10^0 + 10^{-2} + 10^{-4}$ 101.0101
3. $10^6 + 10^3 + 10^1 + 10^{-2}$ 1,001,010.01
4. $10^5 + 10^4 + 10^2 + 10^{-1}$ 110,100.1
5. $10^3 + 10^2 + 10^{-2} + 10^{-3} + 10^{-4}$ 1,100.0111
6. $10^5 + 10^2 + 10^1 + 10^{-1} + 10^{-5}$ 100,110.10001

PAGE 50

Converting Decimals and Fractions

Write the decimals as fractions and simplify.

1. .7 $\frac{7}{10}$ 2. .4 $\frac{2}{5}$
3. .91 $\frac{91}{100}$ 4. .08 $\frac{2}{25}$
5. .26 $\frac{13}{50}$ 6. .702 $\frac{351}{500}$
7. .140 $\frac{7}{50}$ 8. .065 $\frac{13}{200}$
9. .331 $\frac{331}{1,000}$ 10. .092 $\frac{23}{250}$

Write the fractions as decimals.

11. $\frac{6}{10}$ .6   12. $\frac{21}{100}$ .21
13. $\frac{88}{100}$ .88   14. $\frac{64}{100}$ .64
15. $\frac{9}{10}$ .9   16. $\frac{5}{10}$ .5
17. $\frac{197}{1,000}$ .197   18. $\frac{852}{1,000}$ .852
19. $\frac{74}{100}$ .74   20. $\frac{37}{1,000}$ .037
21. $\frac{8}{10}$ .8   22. $\frac{2}{100}$ .02
23. $\frac{7}{1,000}$ .007   24. $\frac{722}{10,000}$ .0722

PAGE 53

Converting Decimals and Fractions

Write the fractions as decimals.

1. $\frac{2}{5}$ .4
2. $\frac{1}{20}$ .05
3. $\frac{3}{8}$ .375
4. $\frac{7}{25}$ .28
5. $\frac{11}{40}$ .275
6. $\frac{1}{2}$ .5
7. $\frac{4}{25}$ .16
8. $\frac{3}{4}$ .75
9. $\frac{4}{5}$ .8
10. $\frac{23}{50}$ .46

PAGE 55

Converting Decimals and Fractions

Write the fractions as decimals.

1. $\frac{1}{4}$ .25
2. $\frac{3}{5}$ .6
3. $\frac{6}{20}$ .3
4. $\frac{2}{25}$ .08
5. $\frac{1}{8}$ .125
6. $\frac{23}{40}$ .575
7. $\frac{10}{25}$ .4
8. $\frac{9}{20}$ .45
9. $\frac{3}{50}$ .06
10. $\frac{2}{125}$ .016

PAGE 56

Multiplying by Powers of 10

Multiply.

1. $.42 \times 10^3$ — 420
2. 2.1×10^{-2} — .021
3. 8.811×10^1 — 88.11
4. 142.8×10^4 — 1,428,000
5. 2.44×10^2 — 244
6. 208.3×10^1 — 2,083
7. $.6452 \times 10^3$ — 645.2
8. 79.05×10^{-3} — .07905
9. 131.5×10^{-2} — 1.315
10. 122×10^5 — 12,200,000
11. 17×10^{-5} — .00017
12. 80.39×10^{-4} — .008039
13. 5.5×10^{-3} — .0055
14. 38×10^1 — 380
15. 143.7×10^0 — 143.7
16. 1.071×10^{-5} — .00001071
17. 0.41×10^2 — 41
18. 16.22×10^{-2} — .1622
19. 203×10^{-3} — .203
20. 14.3×10^5 — 1,430,000
21. 15.1×10^{-1} — 1.51
22. 145.5×10^3 — 145,500
23. 72.7×10^5 — 7,270,000
24. 58.15×10^{-1} — 5.815
25. 8×10^{-4} — .0008
26. 5.68×10^2 — 568
27. 41.9×10^4 — 419,000
28. 13.8×10^{-2} — .138
29. 53×10^1 — 530
30. 6.21×10^0 — 6.21
31. 78.2×10^3 — 78,200
32. 170.4×10^4 — 1,704,000

PAGE 58

Scientific Notation

Evaluate and express as decimal or integer values.

1. 1.2×10^7 — 12,000,000
2. 5.423×10^4 — 54,230
3. 3.45×10^{-8} — .0000000345
4. 9.23×10^{-10} — .000000000923
5. 8×10^{-5} — .00008
6. 4.67×10^8 — 467,000,000
7. 7.1×10^{11} — 710,000,000,000
8. 2.86×10^{-6} — .00000286

Write the numbers in scientific notation.

9. 515,000 — 5.15×10^5
10. 72,600 — 7.26×10^4
11. 340 — 3.4×10^2
12. .106 — 1.06×10^{-1}
13. .0000000302 — 3.02×10^{-8}
14. .00691 — 6.91×10^{-3}
15. 72,000,000,000 — 7.2×10^{10}
16. 52,020,000 — 5.202×10^7
17. 290.3 — 2.903×10^2
18. .00000176 — 1.76×10^{-6}
19. .00024 — 2.4×10^{-4}
20. 416,000 — 4.16×10^5
21. 4,280,000,000 — 4.28×10^9
22. .0258 — 2.58×10^{-2}
23. .000003684 — 3.684×10^{-6}
24. .000381 — 3.81×10^{-4}
25. .000045 — 4.5×10^{-5}
26. 318,000,000 — 3.18×10^8
27. 4,100,000 — 4.1×10^6
28. .0000506 — 5.06×10^{-5}
29. 56,100,000 — 5.61×10^7
30. .012 — 1.2×10^{-2}

PAGE 61

Scientific Notation

Evaluate and express as decimal or integer values.

1. 3.511×10^5 351,100
2. 8.5×10^{-4} .00085
3. 7.1×10^{-7} .00000071
4. 2.23×10^2 223
5. 1.40×10^{-4} .00014
6. 5×10^8 500,000,000
7. 4.3×10^{10} 43,000,000,000
8. 6.412×10^{-5} .00006412

Write the numbers in scientific notation.

9. 1,290,000 1.29×10^6
10. .00000000822 8.22×10^{-9}
11. .0000495 4.95×10^{-5}
12. 771.1 7.711×10^2
13. 483.4 4.834×10^2
14. .00000059 5.9×10^{-7}
15. 6,100 6.1×10^3
16. .0264 2.64×10^{-2}
17. 54,300,000 5.43×10^7
18. 41,800,000,000 4.18×10^{10}
19. .00000000091 9.1×10^{-10}
20. 34,000,000 3.4×10^7
21. 8,306,000,000 8.306×10^9
22. .0000002985 2.985×10^{-7}
23. 1,479 1.479×10^3
24. .129 1.29×10^{-1}
25. 445,100 4.451×10^5
26. 248,000 2.48×10^5
27. 213.5 2.135×10^2
28. .00043 4.3×10^{-4}
29. 8,120,000 8.12×10^6
30. .000000000051 5.1×10^{-11}

PAGE 62

Decimal Addition and Subtraction

Add and Subtract.

1. 8.17 + 52 = 60.17
2. .68 + 29.46 = 30.14
3. 16.9 − .63 = 16.27
4. .32 + 34.19 = 34.51
5. 52.25 − 12.4 = 39.85
6. 3.64 + 83.9 = 87.54
7. 43.5 − 42.73 = .77
8. 73.07 + .11 = 73.18
9. 48.4 − 47.64 = .76
10. 6.12 + 49.7 = 55.82
11. 70.9 − 42.81 = 28.09
12. 31.68 − 23.79 = 7.89
13. 28.95 − 28.7 = .25
14. 60.5 − 52.14 = 8.36
15. 71.97 + 8.9 = 80.87

PAGE 64

Decimal Multiplication

Multiply.

1. .2 × .5 = .1
2. .7 × .9 = .63
3. .5 × .7 = .35
4. .3 × .5 = .15
5. 4 × .7 = 2.8
6. .9 × .3 = .27
7. .6 × 5 = 3
8. .2 × 8 = 1.6
9. .6 × 4 = 2.4
10. .8 × 6 = 4.8
11. .8 × 4 = 3.2
12. .1 × 7 = .7

13. 0.2 × .5 = 3.1
14. 80 × .4 = 35.6
15. 58 × .4 = 23.2
16. 37 × .8 = 29.6
17. 37 × .2 = 7.4
18. 58 × .9 = 52.2
19. 1.8 × 7 = 12.6
20. 71 × .5 = 35.5
21. 78 × .9 = 70.2
22. 3.5 × 9 = 31.5
23. 4.9 × .5 = 2.45
24. 2.6 × .2 = .52
25. 139 × .74 = 102.86
26. 3.04 × 8.6 = 26.144
27. 7.19 × 5.2 = 37.388
28. 38.6 × 2.2 = 84.92
29. 1.87 × 32 = 59.84
30. 78.5 × 6.5 = 510.25

PAGE 66

Decimal Division

Divide.

1. .9)16.65 = 18.5
2. .8)59.28 = 74.1
3. .3)20.04 = 66.8
4. .3)22.53 = 75.1
5. .8)63.76 = 79.7
6. .2)13.84 = 60.2
7. .8)328.8 = 411
8. .4)33.84 = 84.6
9. .3)15.75 = 52.5
10. .9)290.7 = 323
11. .2)10.88 = 54.4
12. .6)14.04 = 23.4
13. 2.6)88.92 = 34.2
14. .21)10.92 = 52
15. .37)22.57 = 61
16. 5.4)25.92 = 4.8

PAGE 68

164   ClayMaze.com

Percent

Write the percents as decimals.

1. 64% = .64
2. 5% = .05
3. 79% = .79
4. 10% = .1
5. 87% = .87
6. 38% = .38
7. 44% = .44
8. 2% = .02
9. 23% = .23
10. 20% = .2
11. 30% = .3
12. 16% = .16

Write the decimals as percents.

13. .01 = 1%
14. .92 = 92%
15. .5 = 50%
16. .29 = 29%
17. .25 = 25%
18. .17 = 17%
19. .08 = 8%
20. .32 = 32%
21. .74 = 74%
22. .88 = 88%
23. .31 = 31%
24. .46 = 46%

Calculate the percentages.

25. 63% of 52 — 32.76
26. 84% of 18 — 15.12
27. 32% of 90 — 28.8
28. 25% of 48 — 12
29. 4% of 55 — 2.2
30. 10% of 42 — 4.2
31. 88% of 87 — 76.56
32. 61% of 73 — 44.53
33. 23% of 21 — 4.83
34. 68% of 53 — 36.04
35. 21% of 92 — 19.32
36. 75% of 46 — 34.5

PAGE 71

Percent

Word Problems

1. Cathy's clothing store normally sells t-shirts for $15. There is a sale for 12% off the regular t-shirt price. What is the cost of the t-shirts during the sale?

    Discount: $15 × .12 = $1.80
    Cost: $15.00 − $1.80 = **$13.20**

2. Mike and Jessica had lunch at a neighborhood restaurant that cost $42. What will be the total payment if they leave a 15% tip for the waiter?

    Tip Amount: $42.00 × .15 = $6.30
    Total: $42.00 + $6.90 = **$48.30**

3. Ten years ago, Erin bought a collectible game card for $5. The value of that card has increased by 75%. How much is it worth now?

    Price Increase: $5.00 × .75 = $3.75
    Current Value: $5.00 + $3.75 = **$8.75**

4. James has a $20 gift card for a game. The game costs $19, but tax is 7%. Will the game card be enough to buy the game? What is the total cost of the game, including tax?

    Tax Amount: .07 × $19 = $1.33
    Final Cost: game price + tax = $19 + $1.33 = $20.33
    The $20 gift card is not enough to buy the game.

5. A local store is having a 20% off sale on shoes. If you want to buy a pair of shoes that normally sells for $75, and tax is 8%, how much will they cost in total? *(Calculate the tax amount after the discount is applied.)*

    Discount Amount: $75 × .2 = $15.00
    Cost with Discount Applied: $75 − $15.00 = $60
    Tax Amount: $60 × .08 = $4.80
    Total Cost(price + tax): $60.00 + $4.80 = **$64.80**

PAGE 72

Order of Operations (PEMDAS)

Evaluate.

1. $3 + 7 \times 5 - 2$ — 36
2. $7 + 15 \div (2 + 3) - 8$ — 2
3. $10 \times (3 + 4) - 8 \times 10 + 5$ — −5
4. $5 \div (2 \times 3 - 1) + 3 \times 11$ — 34
5. $7 + (2 \times 4 - 3)^2 \times 10$ — 257
6. $2 + (2 + 3 \times 4) \div (2 + 5) - 1$ — 3
7. $10 - 8 \times 2^2 \div 4 + 3 \times (8 - 6)$ — 8
8. $3 + 2 \times (3 + 1)^3 - (7 + 4)$ — 120
9. $3 \times (3 \times 5 - 4 \times 2) + (7 - 2 \times 3)^2$ — 22
10. $5 \times (9 - 4 \times 2 + 1)^4 + 10 \div (6 - 1)$ — 82

PAGE 74

Order of Operations (PEMDAS)

Evaluate.

1. $5 - 6 \div 2 + 8 \times 3$ — 26
2. $4 + 3 \times 7 - 10 \div 5$ — 23
3. $7 + (3 - 2 \times 2) + 8 \div 4$ — 8
4. $4 \times (3 + 5) - 6 \div 2 + 7 - 1$ — 35
5. $2 - (5 - 3) + 6 \times 2^2$ — 24
6. $3 - 4 \times 5 + (1 - 9)^2$ — 47
7. $4^2 - (2 - 3 \times 4)^2 + 10 \times 2 + 4$ — −60
8. $6 - 2 \times (3 + 1)^3 + (7 + 4)^2$ — −1
9. $3 \times (2 + 2 \times 3 + 1 \times 2)^0 + (1 - 2 \times 3)^2 - 3 \times 5$ — 13
10. $8 \times 2 + (12 \div 6)^2 - 7 \times 3^2 + (2 \times 2)^3$ — 21

PAGE 75

165   ClayMaze.com

Order of Operations (PEMDAS)

Evaluate.

1. $8 - 10 \div 5 + 7 \times 2$

    20

2. $7 + 4 \times 7 - 12 \div 3$

    31

3. $2 - 8 \times 2 + 10 + 20 \div 5$

    0

4. $15 - (4 + 6 \times 3) \div 11 - 8$

    5

5. $4 + (3 - 5 \times 2) \times (6 - 8) \div 7$

    6

6. $(4 - 5 \times 2) \div (5 - 2^3) + 5 \times 2$

    12

7. $10^2 - (6 \times 2 - 7)^2 + 5^2$

    100

8. $12 + 3 \times (8 - 6)^3 - 4 \times (2 \times 3 - 1)^2$

    −64

9. $(16 - 20 \div 5 + 4) \div (2 \times 5 - 2^2 \times 3)^3$

    −2

10. $4 \times (7 - 6 \div 3 + 5) \div (5 + 8 \times 2 - 4 \times 5 + 1)^3$

    5

PAGE 76

Expressions & Variables

Write expressions for the descriptions below.

1. 21 decreased by x — $21 - x$
2. 8 more than x — $x + 8$
3. m increased by 35 — $m + 35$
4. m divided by 20 — $\dfrac{m}{20}$
5. twice as many as p — $2p$
6. y hundredths — $\dfrac{y}{100}$
7. 15 divided by y — $\dfrac{15}{y}$
8. the sum of 12 and q — $12 + q$
9. x tenths — $\dfrac{x}{10}$
10. the product of 3 and v — $3v$
11. y squared minus 3 — $y^2 - 3$
12. the square root of x — $\sqrt{x}$
13. 2 fifths of m — $\dfrac{2}{5}m$
14. 3 more than (x cubed) — $x^3 + 3$
15. 4 more than twice n — $2n + 4$
16. p fifths minus q — $\dfrac{p}{5} - q$
17. the cube root of v — $\sqrt[3]{v}$
18. z divided by (y cubed) — $\dfrac{z}{y^3}$
19. one half of the square root of the product of x and y — $\dfrac{1}{2}\sqrt{xy}$ or $\dfrac{\sqrt{xy}}{2}$
20. five times the sum of y cubed and 4 — $5(y^3 + 4)$
21. the area of a rectangle whose length is five times its width w — $5w(w)$ or $5w^2$
22. the area of a square whose sides are 8 more than n — $(n+8)^2$
23. the area of a triangle whose base is 4 times its height h — $2h^2$

PAGE 79

Expressions & Variables

Write expressions for the descriptions below.

1. 100 more than s — $s + 100$
2. 5 less than z — $z - 5$
3. two fifths of x — $\dfrac{2}{5}x$
4. p times q — pq
5. x twentieths — $\dfrac{x}{20}$
6. m times the square of c — mc^2
7. y squared plus 71 — $y^2 + 71$
8. f thirds — $\dfrac{f}{3}$
9. the sum of 20 and k — $20 + k$
10. 8 more than (c times b) — $cb + 8$
11. z squared minus 45 — $z^2 - 45$
12. n plus y sixths — $n + \dfrac{y}{6}$
13. twice the sum of x and y — $2(x + y)$
14. 3 divided by (x squared) — $\dfrac{3}{x^2}$
15. y thirds plus t sevenths — $\dfrac{y}{3} + \dfrac{t}{7}$
16. x squared minus 4 — $x^2 - 4$
17. x minus z plus 8 — $x - z + 8$
18. 11 plus y eighths — $11 + \dfrac{y}{8}$
19. the sum of the cubes of x, y and z — $x^3 + y^3 + z^3$
20. b squared minus the product of 4, a and c — $b^2 - 4ac$
21. the area of a rectangle whose length is twice its width w — $2w(w)$ or $2w^2$
22. the area of a square whose sides are 5 units less than t — $(t-5)^2$
23. the square root of the sum of n squared and m squared — $\sqrt{n^2 + m^2}$

PAGE 80

Combining Like Terms

Rewrite the expressions by combining like terms.

1. $3x + 5 - 2x + 5$

    $x + 10$

2. $6y - 2 + 7y + 1$

    $13y - 1$

3. $8x + 4 - 2x - 6 - x$

    $5x - 2$

4. $x + 7 + 5x - 3 + x$

    $7x + 4$

5. $7n^2 + n + 1 - 3n^2 - 4$

    $4n^2 + n - 3$

6. $5x^2 + x + 7 - 8x - 2x^2 + 3x$

    $3x^2 - 4x + 5$

7. $y^2 + 3y - 2 - 4y^2 - 2y + 5y^2 + 1$

    $2y^2 + y - 1$

8. $5x^4 + 3x^2 - 8y + 1 + 5y - 3x^4$

    $2x^4 + 3x^2 - 3y + 1$

9. $x^3 + 5y^2 + 2x - 4x^3 - y^2 + 3$

    $-3x^3 + 4y^2 + 2x + 3$

10. $3n^2 - 5n - 4p - 2n^2 + 7p + 3$

    $n^2 - 5n + 3p + 3$

11. $7y^4 + 3x^2 - x + 3 - y^4 + 5x^2 - 2x - 4x^2 - 2$

    $6y^4 + 4x^2 - 3x + 1$

12. $4n^2 + .2n + 3m + 10 - 7m + 3n^2 + .8n - 8$

    $7n^2 + n - 4m + 2$

PAGE 83

Combining Like Terms

Rewrite the expressions by combining like terms.

1. $4x + 7 - x - 3$

    $3x + 4$

2. $6n - 2 + 7n + 8$

    $13n + 6$

3. $10x - 3x + 5 - 2x + 1$

    $5x + 6$

4. $4x + 1 - 2y - 5 + 3y$

    $4x + y - 4$

5. $x^2 + 5 + 2x - 3 - 2x + 7$

    $x^2 + 9$

6. $-3x^2 - 7x - 4y + x^2 + 8 + 3y$

    $-2x^2 - 7x - y + 8$

7. $8m^2 + 4m - 2 - 5m^2 + 3 + 7m^2$

    $10m^2 + 4m + 1$

8. $4x^3 + 3x^2 - 8y + 6 + 9y - 2x^3 + 11$

    $2x^3 + 3x^2 + y + 17$

9. $2x^2 - 2y^2 - z - 4 + 3x^2 + 3 - 2z$

    $5x^2 \quad 2y^2 - 3z - 1$

10. $-4y^3 - 9x + 6z + 4y^3 + 1 - 4z + 5x$

    $-4x + 2z + 1$

11. $4x^3 - 2z^2 + 4x - y - 10 + 3z^2 + 9 - 4x - 6 - 8x^3$

    $-4x^3 + z^2 - y - 7$

12. $3x^2 + x + 7x - \frac{1}{5}y + 1 + 4x^2 + \frac{3}{5}y - x + 5$

    $7x^2 + 7x + \frac{2}{5}y + 6$

PAGE 84

Evaluating Expressions (Substitution)

Evaluate the expressions with the given values.

1. $3x + 5$ if $x = 2$

    11

2. $6x - 2$ if $x = -1$

    -8

3. $4x + 3y$ if $x = 1, y = 2$

    10

4. $3p - 2q$ if $p = 2, q = -4$

    14

5. $3s - 5 + 6t$ if $s = 2, t = -2$

    -11

6. $2 + 4x - 7y$ if $x = -1, y = 5$

    -37

7. $5x(2x - 4y)$ if $x = 4, y = -3$

    400

8. $2(a^2 + b^2)$ if $a = -4, b = 6$

    104

9. $\dfrac{4y - 5}{2y - x + z}$ if $x = -1, y = 5, z = 4$

    1

10. $\dfrac{2z(4m - 1)^2}{m - 4}$ if $n = 6, m = 3, z = -1$

    242

Express the temperatures below in degrees Fahrenheit using the conversion formula. Use substitution to find the answers.

The conversion formula is: $°F = °C \left(\dfrac{9}{5}\right) + 32$

11. $10°C = \underline{\ 50\ }\ °F$

12. $30°C = \underline{\ 86\ }\ °F$

PAGE 86

Rules of Exponents

Evaluate the expressions. (Use the rules of exponents to help simplify them first.)

1. $7^{10} 7^{-8} = 49$

2. $3^{-7} 3^4 = \dfrac{1}{27}$

3. $\dfrac{4^8}{4^5} = 64$

4. $2^{-56} 2^{61} = 32$

5. $(2^2)^4 = 256$

6. $\dfrac{(-5)^{15}}{(-5)^{12}} = -125$

Rewrite the expressions using the rules of exponents and express without parentheses or negative exponents. Remember: $x^{-n} = \dfrac{1}{x^n}$ and $x^n = \dfrac{1}{x^{-n}}$

7. $x^4 x^5$

    x^7

8. $n^{12} n^{-8}$

    n^4

9. $y^3 y^{-8}$

    $\dfrac{1}{y^5}$

10. $x^2 x^5 x^4$

    x^{11}

11. $\dfrac{z^4}{z^{-4}}$

    z^8

12. $\dfrac{x^{20}}{x^{15}}$

    x^5

13. $\dfrac{b^{-3} b^8}{b^2}$

    b^3

14. $(s^3)^5$

    s^{15}

15. $(x^2)^{-4}$

    $\dfrac{1}{x^8}$

16. $\dfrac{y(y^4)^3}{y^8}$

    y^5

PAGE 89

Rules of Exponents

Evaluate the expressions. (Use the rules of exponents to help simplify them first.)

1. $2^3 2^2 = 32$

2. $3^8 3^{-4} = 81$

3. $(10^3)^2 = 1{,}000{,}000$

4. $\dfrac{11^{22}}{11^{22}} = \dfrac{1}{11}$

5. $4^{-15} 4^{12} = \dfrac{1}{64}$

6. $\dfrac{(278^{32})(278^{-22})}{278^{10}} = 1$

Rewrite the expressions using the rules of exponents and express without parentheses or negative exponents. Remember: $x^{-n} = \dfrac{1}{x^n}$ and $x^n = \dfrac{1}{x^{-n}}$

7. $y^{-2} y^8$

    y^6

8. $x^9 x^7$

    x^{16}

9. $\dfrac{b^{10}}{b^3}$

    b^7

10. $x^n x^{-n}$

    1

11. $z^5 z^{-4} z^3$

    z^4

12. $\dfrac{b^{-2}}{b^{-3}}$

    b

13. $\dfrac{c^8}{c^4 c^{-7}}$

    c^{11}

14. $x^{2n} x^n$

    x^{3n}

15. $(n^5)^{-2}$

    $\dfrac{1}{n^{10}}$

16. $\left(\dfrac{1}{y^{-3}}\right)^4$

    y^{12}

PAGE 90

167   ClayMaze.com

Rules of Exponents

Rewrite the expressions using the rules of exponents and express with no parentheses or negative exponents. *Hint: When possible, simplify complex expressions inside parentheses first.*

1. $(xy)^8$ $x^8 y^8$
2. $(2y)^3$ $8y^3$
3. $\left(\frac{n}{m}\right)^4$ $\frac{n^4}{m^4}$
4. $\left(\frac{10}{s}\right)^2$ $\frac{100}{s^2}$
5. $(6x^4)^2$ $36x^8$
6. $\left(\frac{n^2}{m}\right)^3$ $\frac{n^6}{m^3}$
7. $\left(\frac{2}{x^{-2}}\right)^3$ $8x^6$
8. $(x^2 y^3)^4$ $x^8 y^{12}$
9. $\left(\frac{n^4 m^2}{5m}\right)^3$ $\frac{n^{12} m^3}{125}$
10. $\left(\frac{x^3 y}{xy^2}\right)^2$ $\frac{x^4}{y^2}$
11. $\left(\frac{c^4}{b^2}\right)^{-3}$ $\frac{b^6}{c^{12}}$
12. $\left(\frac{n^{-2}}{m^{-4}}\right)^{-1}$ $\frac{n^2}{m^4}$

PAGE 93

Rules of Exponents

Rewrite the expressions using the rules of exponents and express with no parentheses or negative exponents. *Hint: When possible, simplify complex expressions inside parentheses first.*

1. $(xn^2)^4$ $x^4 n^8$
2. $\left(\frac{y}{t^3}\right)^3$ $\frac{y^3}{t^9}$
3. $\left(\frac{t^2}{5}\right)^3$ $\frac{t^6}{125}$
4. $(s^{-2} r^3)^2$ $\frac{r^6}{s^4}$
5. $\frac{(10n^{-4})^2}{100}$ $\frac{1}{n^8}$
6. $\left(\frac{r^7}{s^{-4}}\right)^0$ 1
7. $\left(\frac{n^3}{m^2}\right)^{-4}$ $\frac{m^8}{n^{12}}$
8. $\left(\frac{4p^2}{m^5}\right)^3$ $\frac{64p^6}{m^{15}}$
9. $(3x^2 y^{-3})^{-2}$ $\frac{y^6}{9x^4}$
10. $\left(\frac{b(b^4)}{c^3}\right)^2$ $\frac{b^{10}}{c^6}$
11. $\left(\frac{n^4 m^{-2}}{m^3 n^2}\right)^2$ $\frac{n^4}{m^{10}}$
12. $\left(\frac{2x^{-2} y}{y^2 x^3}\right)^{-3}$ $\frac{y^3 x^{15}}{8}$

PAGE 94

Distributive Property

Use the distributive property to expand the expressions.

1. $2(x + 5)$ $2x + 10$
2. $5(x - 3)$ $5x - 15$
3. $4(y + 10)$ $4y + 40$
4. $x(x + 3)$ $x^2 + 3x$
5. $x(-x + 7)$ $-x^2 + 7x$
6. $2x(x + 5)$ $2x^2 + 10x$
7. $2n(n + 10)$ $2n^2 + 20n$
8. $2x(x^2 - 1)$ $2x^3 - 2x$
9. $3x(6x^2 - 8x)$ $18x^3 - 24x^2$
10. $-n(n^2 + n - 11)$ $-n^3 - n^2 + 11n$
11. $5x(2x^2 + 3x - 1)$ $10x^3 + 15x^2 - 5x$
12. $x(4x^2 - 3x - 2y)$ $4x^3 - 3x^2 - 2xy$
13. $xy(4x^2 - 3xy + y^2)$ $4x^3 y - 3x^2 y^2 + xy^3$
14. $x^2(2x^2 - 3y - 4xy)$ $2x^4 - 3x^2 y - 4x^3 y$

PAGE 97

Distributive Property

Use the distributive property to expand the expressions.

1. $5(n + 2)$ $5n + 10$
2. $2(x - 4)$ $2x - 8$
3. $3(z - 8)$ $3z - 24$
4. $x(x - 1)$ $x^2 - x$
5. $-3y(y + 2)$ $-3y^2 - 6y$
6. $2x(x - 4)$ $2x^2 - 8x$
7. $5x(x - 5)$ $5x^2 - 25x$
8. $-3(-x^2 - 2)$ $3x^2 + 6$
9. $4x(2x^2 + 3)$ $8x^3 + 12x$
10. $2x(10x^2 + 7y)$ $20x^3 + 14xy$
11. $-7x(2x^2 - 3x + 5)$ $-14x^3 + 21x^2 - 35x$
12. $-x(2x^3 - 3x^2 + 4)$ $-2x^4 + 3x^3 - 4x$
13. $xy(2x^2 + 3xy + 2y)$ $2x^3 y + 3x^2 y^2 + 2xy^2$
14. $xy^2(-x^2 y + 7xy^2 - 2y + 8)$ $-x^3 y^3 + 7x^2 y^4 - 2xy^3 + 8xy^2$

PAGE 98

Distributing / Expanding

Expand the expressions and combine like terms.

1. $(x + 1)(x + 2)$

   $x^2 + 3x + 2$

2. $(x + 3)(x + 4)$

   $x^2 + 7x + 12$

3. $(x - 1)(x + 5)$

   $x^2 + 4x - 5$

4. $(x - 2)(x + 2)$

   $x^2 - 4$

5. $(x + 4)(x - 3)$

   $x^2 + x - 12$

6. $(x + 5)(x + 5)$

   $x^2 + 10x + 25$

7. $(x + 1)(x^2 + 1)$

   $x^3 + x^2 + x + 1$

8. $(x + 2)(x^2 - x)$

   $x^3 + x^2 - 2x$

9. $(x + 2)(x^2 + 2x + 3)$

   $x^3 + 4x^2 + 7x + 6$

10. $(x - 4)(x^2 + 3x - 2)$

    $x^3 - x^2 - 14x + 8$

PAGE 101

Distributing / Expanding

Expand the expressions and combine like terms.

1. $(x - 4)(x + 5)$

   $x^2 + x - 20$

2. $(x - 10)(x + 5)$

   $x^2 - 5x - 50$

3. $(x + 1)(x - 1)$

   $x^2 - 1$

4. $(n + 3)(3n + 1)$

   $3n^2 + 10n + 3$

5. $(4y + 5)(y - 1)$

   $4y^2 + y - 5$

6. $(2x - 1)(x + 3)$

   $2x^2 + 5x - 3$

7. $(3x + 2)(-x + 4)$

   $-3x^2 + 10x + 8$

8. $(n^2 + 2)(n^2 - 4)$

   $n^4 - 2n^2 - 8$

9. $(x + 3)(x^2 + 5x - 2)$

   $x^3 + 8x^2 + 13x - 6$

10. $(x - 5)(2x^2 - x + 1)$

    $2x^3 - 11x^2 + 6x - 5$

PAGE 102

Factoring Expressions

Factor the expressions.

1. $4x + 2$

   $2(2x + 1)$

2. $2x - 16$

   $2(x - 8)$

3. $5x - 15$

   $5(x - 3)$

4. $3y + 9$

   $3(y + 3)$

5. $6n^2 + 24n$

   $6n(n + 4)$

6. $8x^2 - 40x$

   $8x(x - 5)$

7. $12x^2 + 16x$

   $4x(3x + 4)$

8. $4x^2 + 20x$

   $4x(x + 5)$

9. $5x^4y^3 + 10x^5y^2$

   $5x^4y^2(y + 2x)$

10. $2n^4m^3 + 8n^3m^2$

    $2n^3m^2(nm + 4)$

PAGE 105

Factoring Expressions

Factor the expressions.

1. $2x + 8$

   $2(x + 4)$

2. $5x - 10$

   $5(x - 2)$

3. $3n - 21$

   $3(n - 7)$

4. $6x^2 + 10x$

   $2x(3x + 5)$

5. $4x^2 + 16x$

   $4x(x + 4)$

6. $3c^2 - 15c$

   $3c(c - 5)$

7. $2x^3 - 7x^2$

   $x^2(2x - 7)$

8. $12x^4 + 15x^3$

   $3x^3(4x + 5)$

9. $2x^2y^2 + 4xy$

   $2xy(xy + 2)$

10. $3x^3y + 6x^2y^2$

    $3x^2y(x + 2y)$

PAGE 106

169

ClayMaze.com

One-Step Equations

Solve for x.

1. $x + 4 = 20$	2. $4x = 12$	3. $x + 22 = 55$
16	3	33
4. $x - 12 = 37$	5. $3x = 48$	6. $-8x = 120$
49	16	-15
7. $\frac{x}{5} = 20$	8. $12x = 8$	9. $\frac{x}{2} = 15$
100	$\frac{2}{3}$	30
10. $x - 3 = -48$	11. $\frac{x}{3} = -21$	12. $3x = -150$
-45	-63	-50
13. $\frac{x}{7} = -34$	14. $-41 + x = 67$	15. $\frac{x}{4} = \frac{1}{2}$
-238	108	2

PAGE 109

One-Step Equations

Solve for x.

1. $3x = 2$	2. $x + 27 = 10$	3. $15x = 3$
$\frac{2}{3}$	-17	$\frac{1}{5}$
4. $\frac{x}{10} = -20$	5. $17x = 51$	6. $\frac{x}{7} = -44$
-200	3	-308
7. $32 + x = -30$	8. $\frac{x}{5} = 45$	9. $x - 29 = 16$
-62	225	45
10. $x - 14 = 57$	11. $\frac{x}{15} = \frac{1}{5}$	12. $12 + x = 74$
71	3	62
13. $3x = -45$	14. $42x = -14$	15. $8x = -6$
-15	$-\frac{1}{3}$	$-\frac{3}{4}$

PAGE 110

Two-Step Equations

Solve for x.

1. $2x + 1 = 3$	2. $5x - 4 = 6$	3. $3x - 7 = 8$
1	2	5
4. $\frac{x}{5} + 8 = -17$	5. $1 + 7x = 15$	6. $4 + \frac{x}{4} = 12$
-125	2	32
7. $8x - 1 = 3$	8. $\frac{x}{2} + 3 = -5$	9. $6 + 3x = 8$
$\frac{1}{2}$	-16	$\frac{2}{3}$
10. $5 + 3x = 7$	11. $5 + 2x = -45$	12. $\frac{x}{5} - 7 = 23$
$\frac{2}{3}$	-25	150
13. $\frac{x}{3} + 4 = 19$	14. $4x - 11 = 21$	15. $8 + 10x = 12$
45	8	$\frac{2}{5}$

PAGE 112

Two-Step Equations

Solve for x.

1. $4x - 3 = 17$	2. $\frac{x}{5} + 4 = 7$	3. $10 + 2x = 52$
5	15	21
4. $1 + \frac{x}{2} = 0$	5. $8x + 11 = 13$	6. $5 + 4x = 15$
-2	$\frac{1}{4}$	1
7. $5x + 15 = -30$	8. $\frac{x}{11} - 8 = 2$	9. $5x - 4 = 41$
-9	110	9
10. $2 + 6x = 26$	11. $20 + 3x = -10$	12. $5 + \frac{x}{4} = -10$
4	-10	-60
13. $\frac{x}{6} - 9 = 11$	14. $\frac{x}{3} - 8 = 8$	15. $7x - 3 = 53$
120	48	8

PAGE 113

170

ClayMaze.com

Equations with the Variable in a Denominator

Solve for x.

1. $\frac{4}{x} = 2$

    2

2. $\frac{5}{x} = 8$

    $\frac{5}{8}$

3. $\frac{12}{x} = 6$

    2

4. $3 = \frac{6}{x}$

    2

5. $\frac{14}{x} = -7$

    -2

6. $5 = \frac{2}{x}$

    $\frac{2}{5}$

7. $\frac{1}{5x} = 1$

    $\frac{1}{5}$

8. $\frac{9}{5x} = -2$

    $-\frac{9}{10}$

9. $\frac{5}{2x} + 4 = -1$

    $-\frac{1}{2}$

10. $5 + \frac{6}{x} = 7$

    3

11. $8 = \frac{4}{3x}$

    $\frac{1}{6}$

12. $\frac{3}{4x} = -2$

    $-\frac{3}{8}$

13. $\frac{1}{2x} - 4 = 1$

    $\frac{1}{10}$

14. $\frac{2}{3x} + 4 = 9$

    $\frac{2}{15}$

15. $\frac{2}{3x} + 7 = 1$

    $-\frac{1}{9}$

PAGE 116

Equations with the Variable in a Denominator

Solve for x.

1. $\frac{7}{x} = 1$

    7

2. $\frac{3}{x} = -4$

    $-\frac{3}{4}$

3. $\frac{2}{x} = 12$

    $\frac{1}{6}$

4. $8 = \frac{4}{x}$

    $\frac{1}{2}$

5. $\frac{11}{x} = -11$

    -1

6. $1 + \frac{10}{x} = 3$

    5

7. $\frac{3}{4x} = 1$

    $\frac{3}{4}$

8. $\frac{2}{11x} = 10$

    $\frac{1}{55}$

9. $5 = \frac{6}{7x} - 1$

    $\frac{1}{7}$

10. $\frac{8}{x} - 3 = -7$

    -2

11. $\frac{12}{5x} = 4$

    $\frac{3}{5}$

12. $\frac{4}{3x} = 3$

    $\frac{4}{9}$

13. $\frac{3}{4x} + 5 = 2$

    $-\frac{1}{4}$

14. $\frac{4}{7x} - 6 = -10$

    $-\frac{1}{7}$

15. $\frac{1}{5x} + 4 = 8$

    $\frac{1}{20}$

PAGE 117

Combining Like Terms to Solve Equations

Solve for x.

1. $2x + 3 = 5 + x$

    2

2. $3x - 1 = 6 - 4x$

    1

3. $5 + 2x = 3x - 1$

    6

4. $2x - 7 + 8x = 2x + 9$

    2

5. $4x + 2 + x = 1 - 2x$

    $-\frac{1}{7}$

6. $4 + 5x = 3x - 7 + x$

    -11

7. $1 + 5x + 3 = 4x - 8 - 2x$

    -4

8. $3x + 2 - 2x = 2 + 6x - 5$

    1

9. $3 + 2x - 1 + 4x = 8 - 5x - 10 + 7$

    $\frac{3}{11}$

10. $4x - 6 + x + 2 = 10 - 7x + 6 + 2x$

    2

PAGE 119

Combining Like Terms to Solve Equations

Solve for x.

1. $7x - 8 = 3x + 4$

    3

2. $2x - 7 = 9 + 10x$

    -2

3. $4 - 3x = 12 - 5x$

    4

4. $4x - 2 + 3x = 8 - 3x$

    1

5. $5 + 2x = 3 - 7 - 6x$

    $\frac{5}{8}$

6. $3x + 8 - 2x = 10 + 2x$

    2

7. $1 + 3x - 4 = 4x + 7 - 2x$

    10

8. $3x + 2 - x = 5 + 4x + 11$

    -7

9. $4x + 7 + 5x - 1 = 5 + 2x - 3 + 3x$

    -1

10. $5 - 3x + 9 + 4x = 7 - 2x + 3 + 8x$

    $\frac{4}{5}$

PAGE 120

---

171 ClayMaze.com

The Coordinate Plane

Plot and label the points. Indicate which quadrant each one belongs to.

A	(2,3)	Quadrant: I
B	(-2,5)	Quadrant: II
C	(-3,-4)	Quadrant: III
D	(1,-5)	Quadrant: IV
E	(4,1)	Quadrant: I
F	(-3,1)	Quadrant: II
G	(-1,6)	Quadrant: II
H	(5,4)	Quadrant: I
I	(5,-2)	Quadrant: IV
J	(-2,-2)	Quadrant: III
K	(2,-3)	Quadrant: IV
L	(-4,3)	Quadrant: II

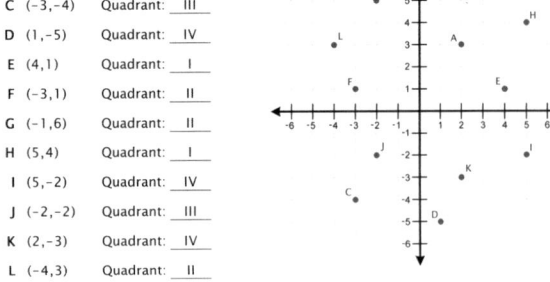

Write the coordinates for the plotted points.

A	(4,-3)	I	(1,-4)
B	(3,0)	J	(-4,-5)
C	(-5,-2)	K	(3,-2)
D	(-2,-5)	L	(1,3)
E	(-2,2)	M	(0,5)
F	(4,4)	N	(-4,4)
G	(0,0)	O	(-2,-1)
H	(-6,1)	P	(5,-6)

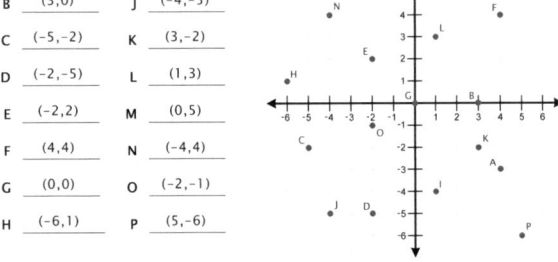

PAGE 123

The Coordinate Plane

Plot and label the points. Indicate which quadrant each one belongs to.

A	(1,1)	Quadrant: I
B	(3,-5)	Quadrant: IV
C	(-5,3)	Quadrant: II
D	(2,6)	Quadrant: I
E	(-4,-4)	Quadrant: III
F	(3,-2)	Quadrant: IV
G	(1,-6)	Quadrant: IV
H	(-2,5)	Quadrant: II
I	(4,3)	Quadrant: I
J	(-4,1)	Quadrant: II
K	(-2,-6)	Quadrant: III
L	(-3,-2)	Quadrant: III

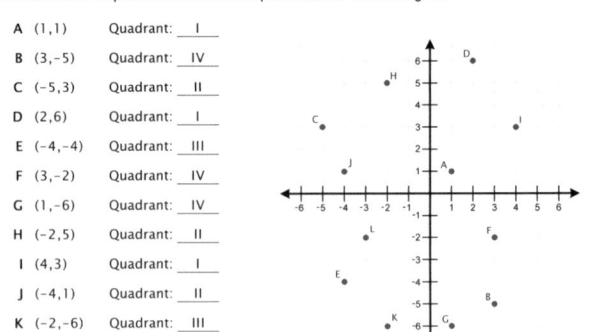

Write the coordinates for the plotted points.

A	(-2,4)	I	(-5,5)
B	(6,2)	J	(-4,0)
C	(2,1)	K	(-3,-5)
D	(4,-4)	L	(1,-2)
E	(-5,-2)	M	(3,4)
F	(3,5)	N	(0,2)
G	(-4,2)	O	(-3,1)
H	(5,-2)	P	(-3,-3)

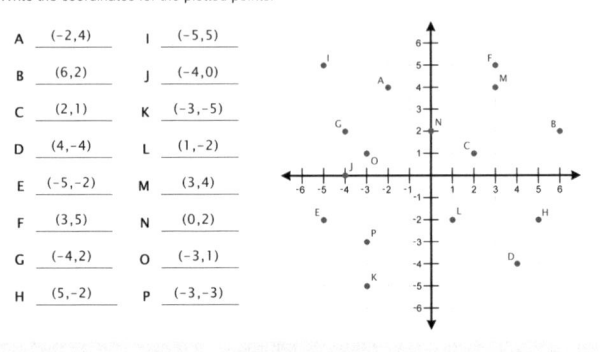

PAGE 124

Distance

Plot the points with lines connecting each pair and find the distance between each pair of points.

A: (2,4) B: (6,4)
Distance: 4 units

C: (-3,-2) D: (3,-2)
Distance: 6 units

E: (1,2) F: (1,-6)
Distance: 8 units

G: (-5,5) H: (-1,5)
Distance: 4 units

I: (-6,-5) J: (-6,4)
Distance: 9 units

K: (-2,1) L: (3,1)
Distance: 5 units

M: (-5,1) N: (-5,-6)
Distance: 7 units

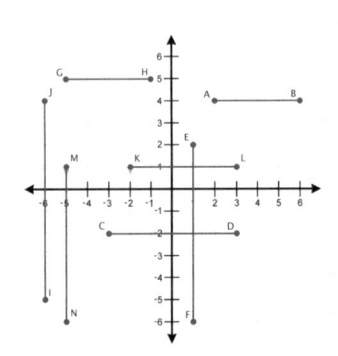

Find the missing points and plot the pairs, drawing lines connecting each pair.

A: (1,3) B: (1,-2)
Point B is 5 units below A.

C: (-1,-4) D: (-4,-4)
Point D is 3 units to the left of C.

E: (-6,5) F: (2,5)
Point F is 8 units to the right of E.

G: (-2,-3) H: (-2,3)
Point H is 6 units above G.

I: (3,-6) J: (-2,-6)
Point J is 5 units to the left of I.

K: (5,2) L: (5,6)
Point L is 4 units above K.

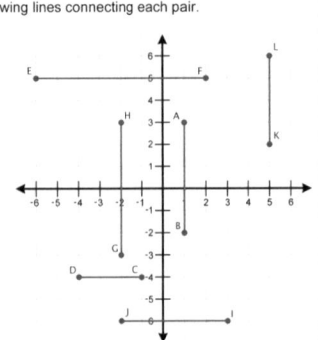

PAGE 126

The Distance Formula

Find the distance between each pair of points using the distance formula.

1. (-5,-2) and (3,4)	2. (2,1) and (5,5)	3. (2,5) and (2,-2)
10	5	7

4. (4,11) and (-8,-5)	5. (-3,8) and (7,8)	6. (2, 2) and (11,14)
20	10	15

7. (-4,4) and (-7,8)	8. (-4,-3) and (5,9)	9. (-2,-3) and (-5,1)
5	15	5

PAGE 129

172

ClayMaze.com

The Distance Formula

Find the distance between each pair of points using the distance formula.

1. (-1,7) and (-1,3)	2. (5,-4) and (-3,2)	3. (2,0) and (-1,-4)
4	10	5
4. (1,-2) and (-4,10)	5. (10,-4) and (-6,8)	6. (1,1) and (-7,7)
13	20	10
7. (-8,-7) and (4,9)	8. (5,5) and (1,8)	9. (-11,4) and (1,-5)
20	5	15

PAGE 130

Midpoint

Find the endpoints and midpoints for the line segments and plot the midpoints.

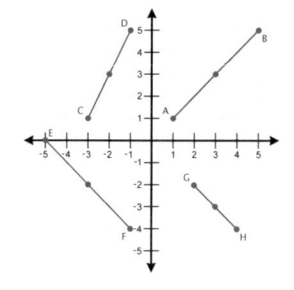

A: (1,1) B: (5,5)
Midpoint: (3,3)

C: (-3,1) D: (-1,5)
Midpoint: (-2,3)

E: (-5,0) F: (-1,-4)
Midpoint: (-3,-2)

G: (2,-2) H: (4,-4)
Midpoint: (3,-3)

I: (1,2) J: (3,-4)
Midpoint: (2,-1)

K: (-2,-1) L: (2,5)
Midpoint: (0,2)

M: (-2,1) N: (0,5)
Midpoint: (-1,3)

O: (-4,3) P: (-2,-3)
Midpoint: (-3,0)

PAGE 133

Midpoint

Find the midpoint for each pair of points using the midpoint formula.

1. (0,-1) and (4,3)	2. (-4,-1) and (2,3)	3. (-5,-1) and (-2,5)
(2,1)	(-1,1)	$\left(-3\frac{1}{2}, 2\right)$
4. (2,-2) and (-3,-4)	5. (1,2) and (4,4)	6. (-3,-5) and (2,1)
$\left(-\frac{1}{2}, -3\right)$	$\left(2\frac{1}{2}, 3\right)$	$\left(-\frac{1}{2}, -2\right)$
7. (-2,-1) and (2,-5)	8. (-4,-1) and (-1,7)	9. (0,4) and (4,0)
(0,-3)	$\left(-2\frac{1}{2}, 3\right)$	(2,2)
10. (-2,-5) and (3,-1)	11. (2,-1) and (-2,-3)	12. (-8,-8) and (8,8)
$\left(\frac{1}{2}, -3\right)$	(0,-2)	(0,0)

PAGE 134

Slope

Find the coordinates of the points and the slope of the lines passing through each pair.

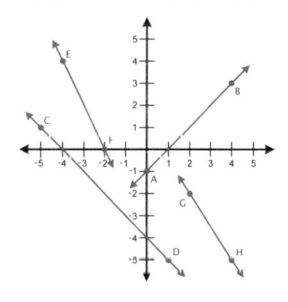

A: (0,-1) B: (4,3)
Slope: 1

C: (-5,1) D: (1,-5)
Slope: -1

E: (-4,4) F: (-2,0)
Slope: -2

G: (2,-2) H: (4,-5)
Slope: $-\frac{3}{2}$

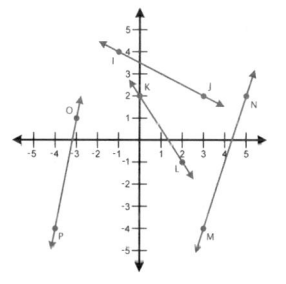

I: (-1,4) J: (3,2)
Slope: $-\frac{1}{2}$

K: (0,2) L: (2,-1)
Slope: $-\frac{3}{2}$

M: (3,-4) N: (5,2)
Slope: 3

O: (-3,1) P: (-4,-4)
Slope: 5

PAGE 137

173

ClayMaze.com

Slope

Plot the points and draw lines passing through each given pair. Find the slope of the lines.

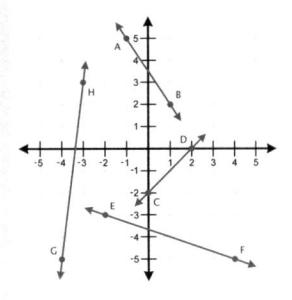

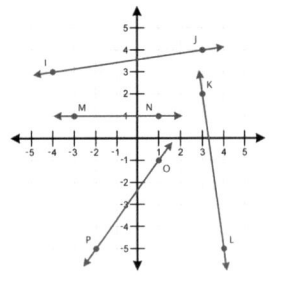

A: (−1,5)   B: (1,2)
Slope: $-\frac{3}{2}$

C: (0,−2)   D: (2,0)
Slope: 1

E: (−2,−3)   F: (4,−5)
Slope: $-\frac{1}{3}$

G: (−4,−5)   H: (−3,3)
Slope: 8

I: (−4,3)   J: (3,4)
Slope: $\frac{1}{7}$

K: (3,2)   L: (4,−5)
Slope: −7

M: (−3,1)   N: (1,1)
Slope: 0

O: (1,−1)   P: (−2,−5)
Slope: $\frac{4}{3}$

PAGE 138

Slope

Find the slope of the line that passes through each pair of points.

1. (1,−4) and (5,−2)	2. (0,−4) and (2,4)	3. (−2,2) and (4,6)
$\frac{1}{2}$	4	$\frac{2}{3}$
4. (4,2) and (3,5)	5. (2,−3) and (0,−7)	6. (1,−6) and (7,2)
−3	2	$\frac{4}{3}$
7. (−4,−5) and (1,−5)	8. (1,8) and (5,0)	9. (−1,3) and (−5,5)
0	−2	$-\frac{1}{2}$
10. (−8,0) and (4,6)	11. (−2,−2) and (2,2)	12. (−1,−1) and (4,1)
$\frac{1}{2}$	1	$\frac{2}{5}$

PAGE 141

Slope

Find the slope of the line that passes through each pair of points.

1. (−5,1) and (−4,−3)	2. (−4,0) and (1,2)	3. (−2,−1) and (2,−7)
−4	$\frac{2}{5}$	$-\frac{3}{2}$
4. (1,4) and (−3,−2)	5. (−1,−3) and (4,−4)	6. (5,4) and (−6,4)
$\frac{3}{2}$	$-\frac{1}{5}$	0
7. (−3,−3) and (4,−1)	8. (−7,4) and (−3,2)	9. (−1,0) and (1,6)
$\frac{2}{7}$	$-\frac{1}{2}$	3
10. (3,2) and (4,5)	11. (5,3) and (−2,−4)	12. (0,1) and (−5,−4)
3	1	1

PAGE 142

Linear Equations and Intercepts

Graph and label the lines, and find their x and y intercepts.

Line A: y = x + 4
x-intercept: (−4, 0)
y-intercept: (0, 4)

Line B: y = x − 5
x-intercept: (5, 0)
y-intercept: (0, −5)

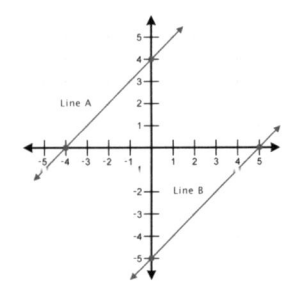

Line C: y = 3x + 3
x-intercept: (−1, 0)
y-intercept: (0, 3)

Line D: y = $\frac{1}{2}$x − 2
x-intercept: (4, 0)
y-intercept: (0, −2)

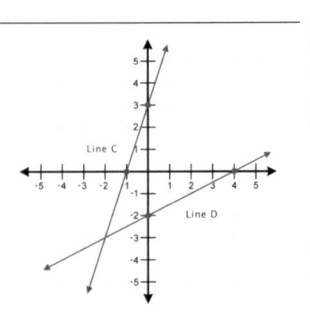

PAGE 145

174

ClayMaze.com

Linear Equations and Intercepts

Graph and label the lines, and find their x and y intercepts.

Line A: $y = -x + 5$
x-intercept: (5,0)
y-intercept: (0,5)

Line B: $y = x - 1$
x-intercept: (1,0)
y-intercept: (0,-1)

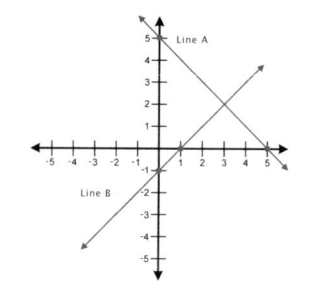

Line C: $y = -2x + 4$
x-intercept: (2,0)
y-intercept: (0,4)

Line D: $y = 2x - 4$
x-intercept: (2,0)
y-intercept: (0,-4)

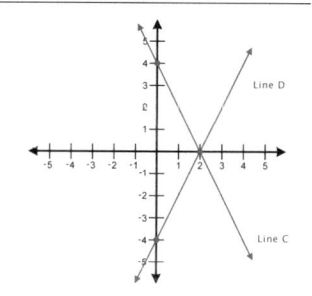

PAGE 146

Linear Equations and Intercepts

Graph and label the lines, and find their x and y intercepts.

Line A: $y = x - 2$
x-intercept: (2,0)
y-intercept: (0,-2)

Line B: $y = -x + 3$
x-intercept: (3,0)
y-intercept: (0,3)

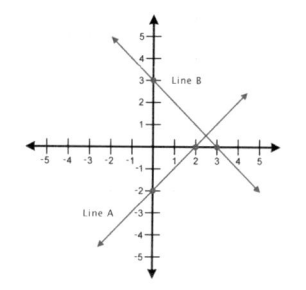

Line C: $y = 5x - 5$
x-intercept: (1,0)
y-intercept: (0,-5)

Line D: $y = \frac{1}{3}x + 1$
x-intercept: (-3,0)
y-intercept: (0,1)

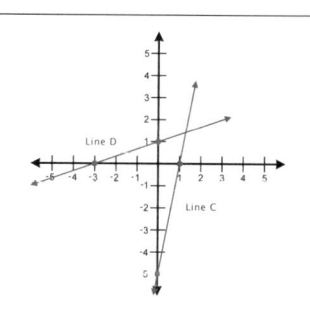

PAGE 147

Linear Equations and Intercepts

Graph and label the lines, and find their x and y intercepts.

Line A: $y = -x + 1$
x-intercept: (1,0)
y-intercept: (0,1)

Line B: $y = 4x + 4$
x-intercept: (-1,0)
y-intercept: (0,4)

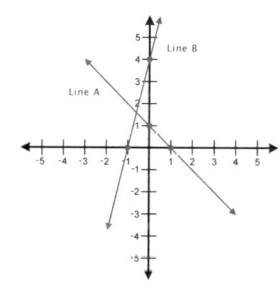

Line C: $y = -\frac{1}{4}x + 1$
x-intercept: (4,0)
y-intercept: (0,1)

Line D: $y = -x - 2$
x-intercept: (-2,0)
y-intercept: (0,-2)

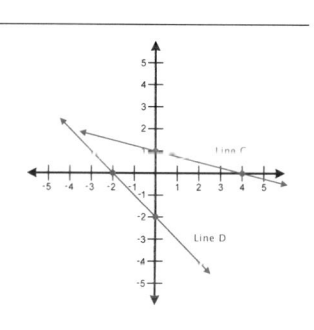

PAGE 148

Slope-Intercept Equations

Find the y-intercept and slope of each line.

1. Line: $y = 4x + 5$
   y-intercept: (0,5)   slope: 4
2. Line: $y = 8x - 3$
   y-intercept: (0,-3)   slope: 8
3. Line: $y = -x + 12$
   y-intercept: (0,12)   slope: -1
4. Line: $y = \frac{2}{3}x + 7$
   y-intercept: (0,7)   slope: $\frac{2}{3}$
5. Line: $y = \frac{5}{2}x + 3$
   y-intercept: (0,3)   slope: $\frac{5}{2}$
6. Line: $y = -6x - 1$
   y-intercept: (0,-1)   slope: -6
7. Line: $y = -4x - 1$
   y-intercept: (0,-1)   slope: -4
8. Line: $y = 3x + 5$
   y-intercept: (0,5)   slope: 3
9. Line: $y = \frac{1}{3}x - 2$
   y-intercept: (0,-2)   slope: $\frac{1}{3}$
10. Line: $y = \frac{7}{4}x + 3$
    y-intercept: (0,3)   slope: $\frac{7}{4}$

Find the equations of the lines given their y-intercept and slope.

1. y-intercept: (0,8)   slope: 1
   Line: $y = x + 8$
2. y-intercept: (0,-3)   slope: 10
   Line: $y = 10x - 3$
3. y-intercept: (0,-1)   slope: 4
   Line: $y = 4x - 1$
4. y-intercept: (0,4)   slope: $-\frac{5}{2}$
   Line: $y = -\frac{5}{2}x + 4$
5. y-intercept: (0,3)   slope: $\frac{1}{2}$
   Line: $y = \frac{1}{2}x + 3$
6. y-intercept: (0,-7)   slope: -1
   Line: $y = -x - 7$
7. y-intercept: (0,-4)   slope: 11
   Line: $y = 11x - 4$
8. y-intercept: (0,2)   slope: 7
   Line: $y = 7x + 2$
9. y-intercept: (0,-2)   slope: $\frac{1}{4}$
   Line: $y = \frac{1}{4}x - 2$
10. y-intercept: (0,1)   slope: $\frac{5}{6}$
    Line: $y = \frac{5}{6}x + 1$

PAGE 151

175   ClayMaze.com

Slope-Intercept Equations

Find the slope-intercept equation (y = mx + b) of the lines shown.

Line A:
y-intercept: (0,-4)   slope: 1
line: y = x − 4

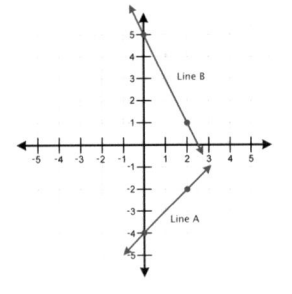

Line B:
y-intercept: (0,5)   slope: −2
line: y = −2x + 5

Line C:
y-intercept: (0,-2)   slope: 5
line: y = 5x − 2

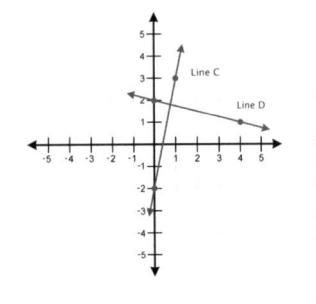

Line D:
y-intercept: (0,2)   slope: $-\frac{1}{4}$
line: y = $-\frac{1}{4}$x + 2

PAGE 152

Slope-Intercept Equations

Find the y-intercept and slope of the given lines and draw their graphs.

Line A: y = 2x − 3
y-intercept: (0,-3)   slope: 2

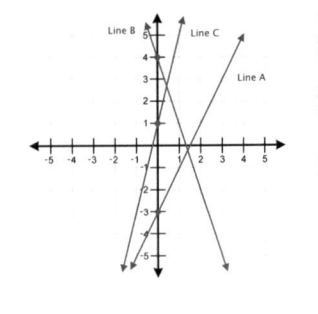

Line B: y = −3x + 4
y-intercept: (0,4)   slope: −3

Line C: y = 4x + 1
y-intercept: (0,1)   slope: 4

Line D: y = $-\frac{1}{5}$x − 4
y-intercept: (0,-4)   slope: $-\frac{1}{5}$

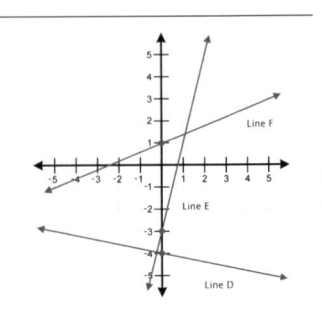

Line E: y = 4x − 3
y-intercept: (0,-3)   slope: 4

Line F: y = $\frac{2}{5}$x + 1
y-intercept: (0,1)   slope: $\frac{2}{5}$

PAGE 153

Slope-Intercept Equations

Find the y-intercept and slope of the given lines and draw their graphs.

Line A: y = 3x + 1
y-intercept: (0,1)   slope: 3

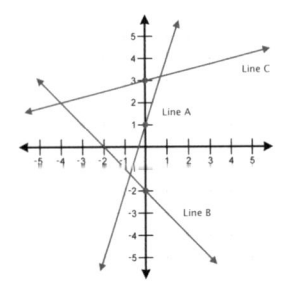

Line B: y = −x − 2
y-intercept: (0,-2)   slope: −1

Line C: y = $\frac{1}{4}$x + 3
y-intercept: (0,3)   slope: $\frac{1}{4}$

Line D: y = $-\frac{3}{2}$x + 4
y-intercept: (0,4)   slope: $-\frac{3}{2}$

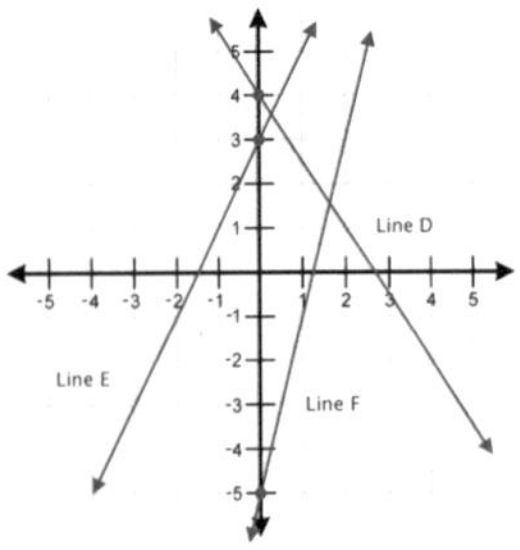

Line E: y = 2x + 3
y-intercept: (0,3)   slope: 2

Line F: y = 4x − 5
y-intercept: (0,-5)   slope: 4

PAGE 154

Made in the USA
Thornton, CO
06/12/25 23:25:48

47902063-950b-4d03-9deb-506ac1aeda76R01